A Journa
Second Sikh War

A Journal of the Second Sikh War

The Experiences of an Ensign of
the 2nd Bengal European Regiment
During the Campaign in the
Punjab, India, 1848-49

Daniel A. Sandford

LEONAUR

*A Journal of the Second Sikh War: the Experiences of an Ensign of the
2nd Bengal European Regiment During the Campaign in the
Punjab, India, 1848-49*
by Daniel A. Sandford

Published by Leonaur Ltd in 2007

Originallt published in 1849 under the title:
*Leaves from the Journal of a Subaltern During the Campaign
in the Punjaub, Sept. 1848 to March 1849*

Text in this form and material original to this edition
copyright © 2007 Leonaur Ltd

ISBN: 978-1-84677-338-9 (hardcover)
ISBN: 978-1-84677-337-2 (softcover)

http://www.leonaur.com

Contents

Introduction

The following pages have already in part appeared in the *Times* newspaper, and are now presented more at large, and in a separate form, in compliance with the wishes of some, who had read them with interest in the columns of that journal.

It is hoped that the importance of the leading events recorded, and the fresh renown which these have added to the British arms, will be deemed to justify the publication of even so slight an attempt to illustrate them; while the fact that this was written without any view to the press, and, from the nature of the case, is published without the youthful writer's privity, will secure the kind indulgence of the reader.

May the same grace be accorded to a father, when he expresses his sense of the mercy that has exempted his own house from sorrows which at this time press so heavily on others. While in the act of tracing these lines, he has received from a bereaved parent a memorial of one—the gallant comrade of his own boy—who died on the field of Gujarat. May the Almighty Himself assuage the anguish He thus permits; and in the hour of our national successes, may we never be oblivious of the blood which purchased them, or, amidst our domestic gratulations, of the mourning relatives of our Hero-Dead.

June 16, 1849

CHAPTER 1

From Subhatoo to Ramnuggur

Subhatoo. Sept. 20, 1848—Ordered to march. All hurry, bustle, and confusion. Half of us haven't got tents—none of us have got any money—everyone is in a whirl of excitement. Words cannot express the trouble, worry, and annoyance of a start; the procuring carriage—settling accounts—paying servants—hunting for a tent, for at present I have nothing but a hat to cover me—raising a little money for the march—writing letters—paying farewell visits—in fact, I am in a state of mind bordering on distraction. The news from Mooltan is, that Shere Singh has gone over to the enemy with seven thousand men; and therefore General Whish was obliged to retreat fourteen miles from the town, to where he has entrenched himself. There has been an attempt at a massacre at Lahore, while Major Lawrence is in an awkward state of siege in Peshawar. Kote Kongra, a hill fort, is also reported to have been taken by four thousand Sikhs. The folly of trusting to these newly-raised troops is now evident; the only force in the place was half a Sikh regiment.

Sept. 24—At daybreak the reveille sounded, and we all formed up in front of the barracks, gave three cheers for Mooltan, and then set out on our march, the band playing, of course, "The girls we left behind us;" marched to Kassowlie to breakfast. Stayed at Kassowlie till half-past three, and then marched down to Kalka, where we arrived at dark, after a march of twenty miles; dined thirty-five in the mess-tent, and slept in an empty one which I happily found; woke in the middle of the night by——, who walks in his sleep, pulling me out by the heels, and insisting I was in his bed. These rascally Sikhs took two prisoners of the 10th Queen's, and hung them up before our pickets, who were too weak to attempt any rescue. Young Lloyd also, a poor ensign, who advanced before his party to parley, was treacherously set on, and cut to pieces. There will be fearful vengeance taken for all this, if we get the better of them; not a man would be spared by our infuriated soldiers, in a case like this. They say we shall require six more European regiments from Bombay, in addition to the force already on its march towards the scene of action.

Sept. 25—Subaltern of the day. Up at daybreak, and inspected the provisions, and marched off the guard; spent the morning looking out for a tent, and procuring carriage; after a great deal of trouble, got hold of two camels—no tent as yet. It is fearfully warm here at present, about ninety-five degrees under cover. Took a bathe in the afternoon at sunset; went round my guards; posted sentries round the camp; went to mess; round again at twelve, and turned in.

Sept. 26—Up early and bathed. We have not yet procured sufficient carriage for half the camp, but hope to get off tomorrow; went out shooting in the morning, and saw nothing but one quail, which I killed; read all afternoon, bathed again, went to mess, and then retired to my tent—a sort of small canvass covering which I managed to purchase cheap, just room for —— 's bed and mine, not very respectable or commodious, but good enough for a subaltern.

Sept. 27—At half-past one the bugles sounded, and the camp, from a state of perfect repose, was instantly all alive—drums beating, mallets going, camels roaring, or groaning, or whatever is the name of the unearthly noise they make when disturbed. In half an hour every tent was struck, and we stumbled through the ground to join the column which was drawn up in the road; pitch-dark, and very close; marched along with our companies some way; then fell to the rear and mounted our horses, and toiled along for about two hours and a half, almost choked with dust, and nearly falling off our saddles every moment, from an overpowering sensation of sleepiness. At last, day broke, and we halted for a quarter of an hour, while the men rested and had their grog. We then proceeded, and another two hours brought us into camp; had a good wash and breakfasted; read all morning; bathed, took a ride on Deception in the evening over the plain—at last I can take a free gallop without danger of breaking my neck; went to mess. The *dâk* came in at dinner-time; no news, except that Shere Singh is looked on with suspicion by Moolraj, and as yet they have not coalesced; two brigades are on their way up from Bombay. Went to bed early, and was unwell during the night from the effects (I believe) of the bad water, which here is execrable.

Sept. 28—Obliged to halt, as we have not yet been able to procure carriage for one bazaar. Fresh disturbances have arisen; the *dâk* is stopped; the Patialah Rajah, who lies right in our route, has risen with a large force. What dependence is to be placed in a native? He was one in whom the government had great confidence, and he held his territories as a fief, being bound to furnish ten thousand men when needed, which he fulfils by furnishing them against us.

Sept. 29—Up at one, marched at two; no one can imagine the discomfort of these first three hours, stumbling along in the dark, wrestling with an overpowering sensation of sleep, in clouds of dust which nearly stifle you, rendering nothing discernible but the tail of the horse before you. Every now and then Somnus gets the best of it, and over you lurch on one side, and are brought up with the muzzle of a musket in your eye; or, riding along unconscious of all around you, hear a snort and a neigh, and bang go a pair of hind legs into your horse's stomach, having got cheek by jowl with the most vicious steed in the regiment. At last day breaks, and you halt for half an hour. Certainly the spectacle that the regiment presents then, is not creditable; every man is powdered over with a thick coat of fine dust, from his whiskers down to his shoes—no recognisable colour about him; all are a uniform dirty hue, and hardly distinguishable from the sandy plain on which they stand, or rather sink. At the halt the men get their grog, (and they want it, poor fellows!) and the officers assemble in groups and discuss sandwiches and coffee, or refresh themselves from their flasks. I stretch my horse-cloth on the ground, light my cheroot, and recline in a state of blissful quiescence until the bugle sounds, when we proceed on our march. Arrived in our ground about seven, a sandy plain, with not a vestige of herbage within sight; breakfasted, wrote journal, and went out shooting; wandered about all morning, but had no luck; dined early. Heat awful—the thermometer mounts to 100° in my tent at noon: what would you think of that in England? One dog went mad, and was shot instantly; he managed to bite——on his hand, but, as he applied burning instantly, no bad effects resulted. Had a very pleasant ride in the evening on Deception: took tea, a walk about the camp, and then went to bed.

Sept. 30—Marched at half-past two; got into our ground at sunrise; breakfasted. Stayed at home in a state of perspiration till three, when I went out shooting; took tea *alfresco*, went to bed; no news; forty men in hospital since we left Subhatoo.

Sunday, Oct. 1—Halted; heat oppressive all day, at one time 110 in my tent; however, I got on very well, barring the inconvenience. Here is nothing to do unfortunately, when we cannot go out, there being only three books in the camp. I write almost all day now, being very fond of scribbling—not that I ever expect to produce anything worth reading, but for my own amusement. With what regret, on a day like this, do I look back on our quiet Sundays at home! How different is everything here; Sunday is no day of rest in India.

Oct. 2—Received a letter from the Mooltan camp; they are still confined to their entrenchments, and have continual skirmishes. They say at Simlah that we are to form one of a brigade under General Gilbert, and march straight to the scene of action; but we may, after all, be sent to the Hazerah country, to fight Chuttur Singh, who will, it is expected, give us lots to do. The Chief says that he does not expect that the campaign will be over for sixteen months yet; it will be hard if, in that time, there fall not a little glory and prize-money to our share. Eight hundred horse, with one of the Sikh Sirdars, joined the enemy the other day, and he promises one thousand more. We marched this morning at four, a short march of eight miles; encamped at Bussi Kusbi, in the centre of an arid plain as usual; heat the same; several of the officers ill. Strolled out with my gun in the morning, but found the heat too great, and returned; spent the day sighing for the breeze, and drinking limes and water—profitable amusement you will say. I likewise passed some time in gazing on certain trees, in a certain picture in my desk, and wishing myself under them, which was also very profitable. Rode Wee Pet in the evening; took tea outside my tent; walked about the camp until nine, and then retired.

Oct. 3—Marched at three, thirteen miles; sand ankle-deep; very hard work for the men, but they went along beautifully; got into our ground at sunrise, breakfasted, and here I sit in the mess-tent. The 4th N. I. are just one march ahead of us in the same route. Too hot to go out; wrote all morning.

Oct. 4—First bugle at half-past two, marched at three; five ladies in their *palkees* passed us on the road, the fair inmates evidently on their way down to a less troubled neighbourhood; encamped at Lusbi Khan ka Surae; went out with some greyhounds in the evening, and had a very fine course after a fawn.

Oct. 5—Marched at three, twelve miles; a continued struggle through knee-deep sand; walked a good part of the way; good exercise for the muscles; reached camp at sunrise, breakfasted, and tried to get a little sleep—no go— my tent is too hot for the balmy god; the sun quite beats through it, and renders it unsafe to stay in it without a hat. My bedstead is sunk half-way up the legs in sand, and everything in the tent is powdered over beautifully with fine particles: how does that suit your ideas of comfort? Finding the sleep a failure, I brought my desk into the mess-tent, and indited an epistle to C——, and wrote rhymes till two, when I adjourned to my tent, and luxuriated in a *mussack* of water. I should like you just to have a look at our camp, as it stands, to take away some of your Byron-derived ideas of the beautiful East. We are pitched on a hard ploughed field, each clod like a flint. Every man you see appears to be drunk, from the impossibility of steering straight, or walking without stumbling; the weary camels are lying in a variety of uncomfortable postures, lolling out their great tongues, and pumping up the water from their intestine wells, with a loud gurgling sound, very unpleasant to the ears. What Byron meant by calling the camel mute, I can't imagine; of all the harsh, horrid, discordant, grating, beastly noises I ever heard, the groans of a camel, being loaded, are the worst. It commences about half-past eight p.m., and lasts, all through the camp, till you go to sleep, which one soon learns to do under any circumstances in India.

Well, so much for our ground; now for the surrounding country. Picture to yourself a scene in the wilderness, all barren, bleak, and sandy to the edge of the horizon, reflecting the rays of the burning sun with a glaring heat that almost puts your eyes out; not a tree nor bladed herbage in sight—nothing but some scanty stunted shrubs, that make you hot to look at them. Oh for the shade of the scented limes! for the refreshing coolness of the evening breeze, rich with the fragrance of the sleeping flowers!—and all that sort of thing—which means, I wish I were out of this, and walking up and down the long walk with my sisters; or what, to my shame be it spoken, I should like a little better, playing cricket in the Lion's Close. Not that I would give up the chance of gaining a ribbon to wear in my button-hole in the coming campaign.

Oct. 6—Up at half-past two; marched at three, twelve miles; got into Loodhiana at sunrise,—beastly hole—nothing but sand. Met the 4th N.I., the 70th, and the 8th cavalry, and some artillery, all encamped here; stayed in all morning; dined, and took a ride about the place—nothing to be seen; sat up till ten in the moonlight. They say here that we are to be brigaded with the 29th and 98th Queen's—if so, we shall form a beautiful European brigade; the 29th and 98th are splendid regiments, and very strong. The 9th Lancers, and 3rd and 14th Light Dragoons are to be formed into a cavalry brigade: and with three troops of horse artillery and two foot batteries, these form the European portion of the reinforcements; the rest will be made up with native corps *ad libitum*. These are only *on-dits;* at present nothing is very certain concerning our future movements.

Oct. 7—Marched at three; lost our way in the dark, the advanced guard going one way, and we the other; consequently the march, instead of being ten miles, was about fifteen, through heavy sand. The men were very much knocked up;—walked most of the way, and arrived in camp rather late. The accounts, in the Delhi, from Mooltan, are not very satisfactory: daily demonstrations; advances and retreats; reconnoitring parties, attacks of the piquets, videttes, and other manoeuvres; but no fighting on a decent scale. I wish those two fools, Moolraj and Shere Singh, were not at loggerheads. I'm afraid they will illustrate the fable of the lion and the two bulls—and we shan't get any fighting after all. Moolraj's men are said to amount to 30,000; if so, he is a fool not to attack at once. The report of the capture of Kote Kongra was one of the many panic-engendered lies which now flit about in shoals, making a man entirely undecided what to believe.

Forces are daily joining the enemy; the whole Punjab is inimical to us, and in case of the least reverse, we should have them about our ears like a swarm out of an upset bee-hive. This state of suspense is very vexatious; and we are rather afraid, too, on account of the weakness of our numbers, of being sent to garrison Jullundur: it would make us frantic. Two ladies were stopped in their *palkees* the other day, *dàking* down to Ferozepore—stripped of everything down to their clothes, and turned back. The roads are not safe, except to large parties. I stayed at home all day; too hot to do anything; even eating was impossible. Went out with my gun in the evening down to the Sutledge; shot a teal; had a pleasant walk along the banks; numbers of fish leaping out of the water at every step; the river is very clear and rapid. Close by here is the field of Aliwal, which I shall go out and see tomorrow evening. The ground we are pitched on at present was the encamping place of the Sikh army. I had a good walk, and came home to the camp as the "Roast Beef" sounded: we always dine late on the halt, but I stick to my early hours, which I find much more wholesome. Had tea with M——outside; the evenings are very pleasant now—beautiful clear moonlight, and blue skies: even this scenery has its charms at night, the bright moonshine glistening on the white sand, and bathing it in a broad sheet of boundless brightness.

Oct. 8, Sunday—Had a good sleep to make up for lost time; stayed in my tent all day; rode out in the evening to the field of Aliwal. Nothing to be seen but a wide plain, and the tomb of a young officer who fell there, and was buried on the spot. Took tea on my return, and went to bed at ten.

Oct. 9—Up at half-past two, and marched at three; road very heavy and dusty. No news, except that they say that Shere Singh has left Moolraj. After dinner, I had a gallop on Deception down to the Sutledge. The river is very rapid here, and there are lots of alligators to be seen. The country is in a very bad state, from the want of rain. The Rajah here says, that, if they do not get some in a few days, there will not be a man left in this part of the country; all will have gone to the foot of the hills, driving their cattle along with them: in fact, there is a great dread of a famine. The heat today was almost stifling: out of curiosity I borrowed a thermometer, and placed it in my tent; immediately it rose to a 110°—ten degrees hotter than it is in the mess tent. Such a season has not been known.

Oct. 10—On duty. Started before the regiment with the advanced guard; marched along till daylight, and then waited for the corps. Halted with them until it was time to take the lead again, and then trudged on into camp; drew up the guard, piled arms, and waited until the regiment passed; presented arms to the Colonel, dismissed my men; inspected the provisions; marched off the guard, saw the ammunition packed, and went to breakfast. Heat intense; wrote part of the morning, put a pillow under the mess-table, and slept the rest: the glass is 104° even there. Bathed at two, dressed, and went to dinner: a hot heavy meal, which no one can eat. Took a ride by myself at sunset over the desert, for really the country about here is nothing else. Very close and sultry; if we do not get rain soon, I'm afraid we shall have no cold season at all. Walked about camp all the evening. These moonlight nights are truly lovely; there is an utter peacefulness, a breathless repose about them, which sinks refreshingly on the languid spirits after the burning heat of the day. The skies, with their myriads of shining stars, are such as, even at home, I don't believe on our most beautiful evenings I have ever seen—a soft, gleaming, milky hue spreads over the firmament, in whose exceeding splendour the stars are almost lost, so vivid is the light which streams over the whole expanse of heaven. I was too excited to rest, and paced up and down the camp till a late hour, when all were sunk in repose. What a time is the calmness of such moments for meditation; how busily, when all else is tranquil, does thought hover over the fields of the past and future, and how deep do we feel the utter loss of the one, and the awful momentousness and obscurity of the other! God make us better for the future, and bring not up the irrevocable deeds of the past against us! After going round the guard for the last time, I retired to bed.

Oct. 11—On rearguard. After the regiment had marched, I had to stay and see all the baggage off the ground; and a nice piece of work I had of it. As soon as I had set one officer's servants to work packing his traps on the camels, and galloped on to another, the fellows would leave their work, and sit down and smoke their *hookahs*; and, on coming round again, I found my men sitting on the ground, and things just as I left them. I then adopted a new method, waiting by the camel until each separate establishment was under weigh, and had left the ground. I then went on to another. In this manner, after a good hour's worry and abuse, I managed to get the ground clear. I then marched off the guard, and we walked along merrily till daybreak, when I halted for twenty minutes; spread my horse-cloth on the ground, and enjoyed that which getting up every morning at half-past two, and a hot march, makes particularly refreshing—*viz.*, a full-length recline on the sand, and a fragrant weed. The men piled arms, and sat or stretched themselves on the ground in groups, amusing themselves with passing their unsophisticated comments on the passers by. Poor fellows! They are in great spirits at the prospect of seeing service at last: after so many disappointments, it will be cruel if they are not gratified—that is, if there is anything to be done.

When I thought we had rested long enough, I gave a last stretch, gathered up my limbs and proceeded to camp, which we reached a little after sunrise. Went to the colonel's tent, and reported all correct, answered all his questions—he is very strict, and pulls you up for the least omission;—breakfasted; spent the day as usual; heat worse than ever. General Whish has retired seven miles further from Mooltan; no news of importance; they say that Lord Dalhousie has permission either to annex the whole of the Punjab, or to withdraw altogether from it. I hope they will annex it, as there will be lots to do, and a large augmentation of the army. At any rate we must thrash Moolraj. Poor Mrs Lawrence failed in her attempt to reach Lahore; she was seized, stripped of all she had with her, and sent back to her husband, who was anxiously waiting to hear of her arrival in safety. He, poor fellow, is left in his fort with none but Sikh troops for his garrison, and a reward offered for his head by Chuttur Singh. The place he is in, too, has no great strength, and must fall before a determined attack: I wish they would send us to relieve him.

Oct. 12—Marched at three; so close we could hardly breathe; obliged to halt twice in a short march of nine miles. Wrote all morning; bathed; dined, and went out, riding in the evening with———; saw a paria, and gave chase. I took the lead on Wee Pet, and we were flying along at full speed, the dog just ahead, when all of a sudden my horse plumped up to his knees in a morass, and nearly fell; but a strong pull, and his own stout little legs, carried him through. I looked round, and beheld poor ———, horse and man, lying in a heap in the centre; the rider shot well ahead, and almost buried in the bog, and his horse floundering along on his nose and knees: however, no one was much hurt, either horse or man. Caught the horse, picked up the rider, and continued the chase; but doggie was too far ahead, and could not be overtaken. Came back to camp, laughing all the way at poor ———, who was one moving mass of mud, from the nose down to the boots. Spent the evening strolling about the camp, and talking disconsolately about my future prospects with T———, who is a great chum of mine.

Oct. 13—Marched at three; a slight variety, in the shape of low briary jungle, relieved the tedium of the road. Arrived in camp very early, and were entertained with a dust storm until twelve—very common occurrence here, I believe. Wrote all day, it being the only thing I could do, and in the evening strolled out for about six miles with my gun, saw nothing, and had my walk for my pains. Evening spent as usual; slept outside, and sent my tent ahead; awakened in the middle of the night by a dust storm sweeping over me, and saw my hat quietly trundling out of camp. Went to sleep again, and woke up with a cold.

Oct. 14—Marched at half-past three, very chill until sunrise; halted about half a mile from Ferozepore, adjusted our plumage, and then marched into the station, colours flying, and the band playing splendidly. Drew up in line before our camp, and saluted the insignia. The regiment looked very well, and a lot of people rode out to meet us, my old friend S—— amongst the rest. In the evening rode on the course, and dined at the 31st mess. Things seem to be going on very well; the whole country between this and Lahore has risen. There are large bands of hostile cavalry infesting the road, under some robber chief or other, and they say that the Sikhs are determined to make one last effort: the Chief is expected down with all speed, and there seems a prospect of lots to do. And now, as for Ferozepore. Such a hole as it is!—A row of dreary, dusty bungalows and barracks, looking out disconsolately and sourly on the bleak plain. There is not the faintest suspicion of a tree, or a vestige of herbage, for ten miles round; my grass-cutter has to go a day's journey to get fodder for the horses. Grain, too, is awfully dear: how the poor brutes are to live, I don't know. I am trying to sell both mine, and will walk like the men; I don't see why I shouldn't, as well as they. At any rate, anything is preferable to seeing the brutes starve before my eyes, as must shortly

21

be the case if things do not take a better turn; and what makes it the more aggravating is, the staying here doing nothing, whilst others are reaping honours under the walls of Mooltan. But as long as hope continues to smile, as long as home glimmers, however faintly in the distance—as long as there is the remotest chance of battles, prize-money, distinction, or an honourable death, I shall keep up my spirits, and never say die, as long as my head is above water. When *that* is impossible. . . . So——has been living in clover lately, basking in the smiles of beauty. Happy fellow! On me no smiles beam sunshine, no eyes look welcome when I come. I am a poor, disregarded, snubbed, and devil-may-care sub. That is, I believe, what is called being independent—*viz.*, having to pay your own tailor's bills, with nothing to pay them with; having to feed yourself, with no means to procure food; and having to be answerable for your own actions, with no discretion to govern them. I am, however, in capital health, and hope to continue so, as this is the only thing we poor soldiers can afford to keep.

Sunday, Oct. 15—Stayed in camp all day; much tormented with the dust, which is so fine that the slightest puff of wind raises it in clouds. There is a large force at present encamped here. All the reinforcements for Whish have been countermanded, as they dare not leave the station unprotected. There is an encamping-ground marked out for twenty thousand, most of them on their way up.

Oct. 17—Our old friends the artillery are encamped here. Rode over to their camp, and took a cup of tea with B——. Nothing going on at Mooltan: a lot of wine stores fell into Moolraj's hands the other day. He kept the brandy, but not being able to appreciate the beer, which the niggers call *mila panee,* dirty water, he allowed it to proceed to our camp. There is a good story told of him, whether true or not I can't say: his followers boned a lot of hermetically sealed provisions in tin cases, and not having seen anything of the sort before, he mistook them for canister-shot, and fired nothing from his guns for three days but fresh lobsters, pickled salmon, potted shrimps, and other delicacies, supplying the whole British camp with a shower of the freshest English provisions. We have been put into a fresh brigade with the 70th and 45th N. I. The 29th have suffered very much: they left Kussowlie 1300 strong; and out of that have now 400 in hospital. Colonel Godby has command of our brigade. The 69th N. I. move down to the bridge of boats today to protect it, as there is great chance of an outbreak there. S——dined with me in the evening, and thus closed the events of the day.

Oct. 18—The mornings now are getting very cold, though the day-heat is as bad as ever; nothing of consequence occurred all day. I wish the old Chief would look sharp, and come down; there will be no fun until he arrives.

Oct. 20—Eckford's brigade and the artillery marched this morning for Mooltan; Lord Dalhousie is on his way up.

Oct. 21—How little we know about our movements. Yesterday not one of us expected to move for a fortnight at least, and now we are ordered off on Monday morning with the 3rd Dragoons and 9th Lancers, and our brigade—namely, ours and the 70th N. I., who took the place of the 45th, who have not arrived yet, to effect a junction with the forces at Lahore; so we are likely to have the first of the fighting after all. Stayed at home all day, and had a game at cricket in the evening with C—— and T——, and half-a-dozen niggers as fags. A farewell party to —— was given tonight. The evening passed off very pleasantly. Colonel, I mean Brigadier, Godby proposed his health, and he returned thanks in a very sincere, if not brilliant speech. After that, we hoisted him up in his chair, and told the band to strike up, and carried him round the table in state. Lots of loyal toasts were afterwards proposed—"The Army of the Punjab, John's own brigade, The Army of Mooltan—and "The girls we left behind us:" they were all enthusiastically drunk, but none, I need scarcely say, like the last. Eckford's brigade has been recalled. There is a report that the enemy are advancing on the capital, which is glorious news for us. What is in store we cannot say, but the brigadier, our late colonel, is in great spirits, and rubbing his hands at the idea of gaining more laurels. God bless you for your anxious love! I trust He will protect me in His mercy, however unworthy, and that your prayers for me may not be in vain.

Oct. 22—Stayed in camp all day; very dusty, and lots of the phenomena called *devils* going about. What is here called a *devil* is an immense pillar of dust whirling round and round, and catching up everything in its progress; it is in shape like a pyramid, reaching often more than half a mile in height, very black and thick towards the bottom, but light and vapoury towards the apex. Whatever touches it immediately breaks it up, so you may imagine the pleasure of one of them walking through your tent. I have seen six or seven wandering about the plain at the same time, and with very little wind. So dear little E——is growing up quite a hero! You had better educate him for this country, he would get on splendidly; only, if you ever think of such a thing, you cannot begin too early. The studies appropriate are, first of all, mathematics, fortification, and arithmetic, as far as it is connected with keeping accounts. A thorough knowledge of the latter is very necessary: not any of your intricate forms of double entry, and all that sort of thing, but enough to enable him to keep his own accounts accurately, and take the management of any public office that may offer. Let him learn French thoroughly. Latin and Greek are only accomplishments out here; and though every gentleman should of course have a knowledge of them, they will be of no use to him in his profession. Confine his education to what is called useful knowledge—*viz.*, history, geography, composition, arithmetic, and modern languages; in these he cannot be too well up. Of course, any other accomplishments will be of advantage to him, but these should be his chief studies. Let him be taught to act and think for himself early, and learn to consider himself answerable for his actions. But all this is sending coals to Newcastle, I well know, especially as I suppose you would just as soon think of flying, as of parting with the little fellow; and I myself am doubtful whether I would really advise it. The advantages are these,—to any one who gets an appointment, be he the veriest dolt that ever breathed, it is a provision for life, after he has once got over the first two years. To an intelligent and *industrious man,* with a little interest, it is a splendid opening to future preferment, sooner or later; but it carries with it this drawback, that of perpetual exile from your native land, and all you love best. You cannot attain any post of eminence under twenty years, or even realise sufficient to enable you to live comfortably at home; and if you obtain a good appointment, you cannot without loss throw it up, and take your furlough even. You don't get your bread till you have no teeth to eat it with; you spend the flower of your life in a foreign land, and return home with the means, but not the power of enjoyment. A man, I should say, would be happier if he could realise a competence in England, than revelling in wealth in this country—but enough of this.

Oct. 23—Up at half-past three; marched at half-past four; got clear of Ferozepore, and proceeded about four miles, when we had to ford a broad stream. One of our men got into a small quicksand, and had great difficulty in extricating himself, amidst the roars of the regiment, which must have been very aggravating to him as he was floundering about. Halted on the other side for half an hour, and then marched on till we reached the Sutledge; crossed the bridge of boats, and entered the Punjab, the renowned land of the five rivers; and a very barren, ugly-looking land it is at present. Got into camp rather late, and encamped with the 70th on our front, and the cavalry and artillery on the rear and flanks. Went over during the day to the camp of the 5th Light Cavalry, who are out here for forage; had a long talk with T——; dined, and played at cricket in the evening.

Oct. 24—Marched at half-past four. A camp-follower was attacked and robbed during the night; he is much wounded, and not likely to recover. The country is much infested with thieves; there is a celebrated tribe of them, who inhabit the banks of the Sutledge, and who are very expert at their trade. Encamped at Kussoor; advised not to leave camp, as there are several strong bands of robbers prowling about the vicinity. Stayed in my tent all day reading, and played cricket in the evening.

Oct. 25—Marched at half-past four; short march; nothing worth recording.

Oct. 26—Marched at half-past four—eight miles; bitter cold; came on to rain violently after breakfast. Stayed in our tents all day, except when, as officer of the day, my duties compelled me to go and get drenched. After dinner it cleared up, and we had a game at cricket. At sunset I posted the sentries round the camp, and played the flute till nine, when I visited the guard, and turned in.

Oct. 27—Up at half-past one; a despatch had come in the night, ordering our immediate arrival at Lahore; so we had to make a forced march of it, and knock the two into one. Being the officer on rearguard, I had to stay behind, and see all the baggage off the ground, which took me about an hour and a half. I then followed the corps with my company; did the twenty miles in beautiful time, and arrived in camp soon after the brigade. We are pitched about two miles from this mighty city, (Lahore,) but as we move on across the Ravee river tomorrow, I shall have no time for sight-seeing. Rode over to cantonments in the evening, to get a few things I wanted. Dined late, and turned in. The troops here are constantly under arms from alarms of the enemy, who make repeated night excursions across the river, and retire again on being menaced.

Oct. 28—Marched at five; passed through cantonments with the band playing, and proceeded about five miles down to the Ravee, which we crossed by the bridge of boats, and encamped about half a mile on the other side. Here with our brigade, and the cavalry and artillery, we are to form a sort of army of defence. Breakfasted and retired to my tent, where I spent the morning reading, and was reclining quietly on my bed, when I thought I heard an unusual uproar in the camp—mounted orderlies galloping about, and people inquiring what was the matter; so I turned out, and found that a party of the enemy had walked off with fifty of our camels, while out grazing, and had killed a few of their drivers. The cavalry were out instantly in pursuit, and the grenadier company was ordered to be under arms, and ready at a moment's notice. After a couple of hours the cavalry came back with most of the camels, which, on being pursued, the enemy had left, and taken to their heels. They have been very bold and annoying lately, and attacked a little fort the other day on the river, in which there was only a few of the Durbar troops, who were quietly massacred. Since then, there has been always a guard of sepoys and a European officer there. They likewise attempted to burn the bridge of boats; and succeeded in destroying two of the boats, but were beaten off. We caught a spy in camp today, and packed him off to Lahore to Sir F. Currie—as yet we have a very vague idea of the force or locality of the enemy. Two thousand are said to be hovering about in the vicinity, and we are obliged to keep a sharp look-out. Chuttur Singh has, they say, no less than 50,000 followers, but he is not within ten marches. Shere Singh likewise has a large force of rabble. If they don't show some fight with all this, they are not worth much. Poor——is dead! How common are these sad incidents in a soldier's life, and, alas! how little regarded! No news from Mooltan; played at cricket; dined and turned in; but all ready to turn out again, if there should be the least alarm: none however took place.

Sunday, Oct. 29—All quiet; prayers read by the commanding officer in camp. The weather has become very pleasant now, after the rain we had the other day. Rode over to Lahore in the afternoon, and hunted out the quarters of F—— B——. You remember him, I dare say. Found him living in one of the city gates, where his regiment is quartered; had tiffin with him, and a talk about old times, and rode back just before sunset—as it is not advisable to be out after that time, unless you want your throat cut.

Oct. 30—Out on parade. All the officers have been ordered to rub up their sword exercise, and a very amusing spectacle it was. Had to stay in camp all day, as my company was in picket, and all the officers belonging to a company on duty have to be ready at a moment's warning. Spent a very stupid day in camp. The nights are bitter cold now, but in the daytime the sun still continues very hot.

Oct. 31—Parade in the morning. After breakfast crossed the river and rode into Lahore to play cricket. Had a very nice game with a lot of officers from the different corps there, spent a very pleasant day, and met an old schoolfellow. H——and C——must remember him—B——by name: he boarded at P——'s. He seems a very nice fellow, belongs to 46th N. I. Returned to camp in the evening—went to mess. A party of the 46th dined with us,—as genial a set of fellows as I wish to see—lots of singing and fun after dinner. Had a long chat with B——on old times, and spent a very happy evening. You have no idea how pleasant it is to meet anyone you know in this dreary land, and recall with him old scenes of past enjoyment. Tell Mr P——, if you see him, that he wished to be remembered.

Nov. 1—Parade after breakfast. Rode into Lahore, and spent the day with B——; returned to camp in the evening.

Nov. 2—Up early in the morning, and walked over with one or two other men to Jehengire's tomb. It is a splendid building, and well repaid us for our long walk. The whole dome, which is of immense size, is composed of the most beautifully polished marble, of various colours. Read the description at the beginning of Esther, and you will have a good idea of it, bating the gold and silver. There was a miserable self-mutilated Faqueer at the gate, with his legs, *all-no-how*. There are swarms of these disgusting fanatics, in every shape of unnatural deformity, to be seen at every Hindu place of worship, and a very profitable thing they make of it: the respect they excite among the natives reminds me of the jolly old days of the grey Friars. Saw all that was to be seen, and returned to camp. Lost my breakfast, rode into Lahore, *tiffed* at the artillery mess with B——, who has followed us to Lahore, and got posted to a battery here. Played cricket after dinner, and then went over to inspect a batch

29

of young Arabs with ——, mounted on a very showy little grey, perfectly unbroken; and a very pretty piece of work he gave me. For the first two minutes, I did not know whether I was on the ground or in the air; however, at last I mastered him, to the great admiration of the Arab merchant. Rode the little horse back to camp, —— rode another, and a mad tear we had of it. When we arrived there, we found that we were to march in the morning to meet the enemy, who are said to be only thirty miles off.

Nov. 3—Marched at five. Walked the first twelve miles, as I have lent both my horses, being unable to feed them myself. But at last, as good luck would have it, I got hold of a beautiful young Arab, full of blood and spirit, belonging to a friend, and rode the remaining four miles of the march. It was awfully hot; we didn't arrive in camp until twelve, and got nothing until near two. Pleasant work campaigning! It reads very pretty in one of Charles Lever's novels; but experience of it dispels the charm. They say that we shall meet the enemy tomorrow: they have seized on a small town, where all our commissariat stores for the army were laid up, and we are going to drive them out. Our force consists of our own regiment, the 70th N. I., 14th Dragoons, 5th Light Cavalry, and 12th Irregulars, one battery, and three troops of horse-artillery.

Nov. 4—Marched at daybreak, the artillery in front, the cavalry on the right and left, and the 70th on our rear. At one time we expected to have a fight before we got into camp, but we saw no enemy; and after a weary march of twenty miles in a scorching sun, we reached our encamping ground about twelve o'clock. Had to wait another hour on the bare plain before our tents came up; and up to this hour, which is nearly 4 p.m., I haven't tasted food. We march directly after dinner, as they say the enemy are close ahead, and intend to make a stand of it,—so good-by for the present, as I feel the cravings of hunger very strong, and I can't fight on an empty stomach.

Evening—Our march countermanded—heaven knows why. The enemy are five thousand strong—nine miles ahead, in a fort; and they say they will wait for us. If they do, it will be sharp work, as cavalry will be no good there: all the fighting will devolve on the infantry. Got dinner at five, and, feeling rather tired, turned in soon after sunset.

Sunday, Nov. 5—Marched at four. How our men strode along! The —th, who followed in our rear, were literally obliged to run, to keep up with us. Marched nine miles, and came in sight of the fort; halted, and sent a squadron of the 12th Irregulars on to reconnoitre. Two strange flags were floating on the ramparts, and we thought that all was right, and we were in for a good fight. I dare say, when the campaign is over we shall not be quite so eager. Imagine our disgust when we found that the enemy had retreated on the Chenab, and the forts were held by a friendly force. Marched five miles more, and weary work it was in the hot sun: my face is burnt to a cinder, and crawling along on horseback makes you feel it all the more. As for walking, it is fearful work, after the sun has risen. How often have I wished, as I toiled along ankle-deep in sand, that my tailor had paid less attention to *fit* and more to comfort. But the worst part of it is, having to wait an hour after you reach your ground, with no protection whatever from the sun, and nothing to sit down on, except the heated ground. I have put John Company and myself down as quits from this day; whatever extra work he takes out of me, I shall consider him my debtor. Got into our ground at ten, tents up at eleven, breakfasted at twelve. The enemy are collected at Wuzeerabad, about twenty miles off, in force—some say

31

25,000, some 30,000—and as it is thought hardly prudent to attack them with 4,500, we are to halt here, until reinforced by Eckford's brigade.

Nov. 7—Marched at five o'clock. Intelligence arrived in the night that Shere Singh was marching on Lahore by the Ramnuggur road,—so made a cut across the country, altering our intended route, to intercept him. Marched thirteen miles, and halted at eleven, about ten miles from Ramnuggur. Heard guns distinctly towards the end of our march—though, what the deuce they were firing at, we could not make out. The sound evidently came from Ramnuggur, where our spies say that Lall Singh is at present with three thousand men and twenty-four guns, Shere Singh advancing in his rear with eighteen thousand men. Got breakfast at one, and are ordered to hold ourselves in readiness to march again at four.

Evening.—March countermanded. Went to mess, and was sitting after dinner, when a mounted nigger brought the news into camp that the enemy were coming down upon us, and intended to make a night-attack. Everyone was instantly on the alert—pistols loaded, swords laid handy, and all ready to turn out at a moment's warning. Went to bed at ten, and the night passed off without anything occurring.

Nov. 8—Up early, heard guns from Ramnuggur, and found out afterwards that it was a salute fired by the enemy to hail the arrival of Shere Singh, who has joined with his whole force—so that there is now a body of 20,000 men within eleven miles of us. General Cureton has received strict injunctions not to act on the aggressive, nor to advance an inch until the arrival of the Chief, who, they say, will arrive on the 15th, with a large army. Eckford's brigade joins us tomorrow. From Mooltan we hear that Moolraj made a sally the other day, and was beaten back: no operations, however, will be commenced until the 1st of January. Went to mess, and then walked out to see E——, who was in outlying picket, about a quarter of a mile from the camp. It was a beautiful moonlight night—very cold—and I enjoyed my walk. Found him bivouacking under a tree, with his men wrapped up in their greatcoats, and strewed about the ground sleeping, until their turn for standing sentry came round. And on all sides were dark muffled figures, pacing slowly up and down—the moonbeams gilding their polished bayonets; and every now and then the peremptory challenge of "Who comes there?" arrested some poor nigger, who was quietly strolling into camp, in the innocence of his heart, and found himself disagreeably undeceived, and nothing for it but to sleep in the open air. Sat with E——, talking for about two hours, and then returned to camp.

Nov. 9.—Moved our ground about a mile, to make room for Eckford's brigade, which came in about seven, consisting of three native corps, and one battery—so we are now pretty well off—the 31st, 56th, and 73rd. There is a rumour today that Gholab Singh has gone over to the enemy; if he has, we shall have as much to do as we can manage. So much the better for us. Holmes, of the 12th Irregulars, was out with his patrol, when they had a rencontre with the enemy. He had only eighty men with him, and yet he rode backwards and forwards before the party, who consisted of four hundred horse, and offered them battle. But they wouldn't come on. Just as well for him that they didn't! He is a brave fellow, however, and got his present command by a piece of daring at Sobraon: he swam his horse over the river in face of the enemy, spiked a gun, and swam back again, under fire all the while, and the river running like a sluice. Nothing more happened all day. We are all expecting to be attacked, and all are in readiness. Went to mess, and walked about some time afterwards, enjoying the deliciously clear moonlight.

Nov. 10—Up early. The brigade was out on parade, and we had a lot of manoeuvring and running about. Breakfasted, wrote, and then walked over to the 31st; *tiffed* there, and was sitting quietly afterwards listening to their band practising, when we heard a great uproar, and several sepoys came rushing past the tent, crying out—"An attack! An attack! the enemy are coming down!" Everyone was out of the tent like magic. I returned for my cap, which I had forgotten, and made all speed to my own camp. The alarm sounded as I was on my way, and all the troops turned out, and stood to their arms in an incredibly short space of time. Threw off my shooting-coat, pulled on a red jacket, buckled on my sword, and rode out with———to see what was going on. I wish I hadn't. I started off at a brisk pace, and my horse ran away with me over rough ground about three-quarters of a mile. Pulled him up at last by the outlying dragoon picket, and found he had sprung the back sinew of his fore-leg, and was dead lame. My luck again! I shan't be able to sell him now. The alarm turned out to be a false one after all, and I had nothing for my trouble, but a lame horse. Poor little pet! I'm afraid I shall have to shoot him. Returned to camp very much disgusted, as you can suppose—"I never loved a tree, &c." Went to mess, and spent a very miserable evening; but, thank goodness, I'm a bit of a stoic, and soon came to the conclusion that what's done cannot be helped. Still I felt very uncomfortable, when I went to have a look at the poor fellow before going to bed: saw that his bandages were all right, and kissed him, and wished him goodnight.

Nov. 11—Nothing worth mentioning occurred in our camp, except that two miserable camp-followers were cut up, and brought in dead from a neighbouring village, where they had gone for supplies. We hear from Mooltan that they had a brush the other day—three or four officers killed, and sixty men wounded, names as yet not known. Chuttur Singh had taken possession of Peshawar, and seized twenty of our guns; Shere Singh has withdrawn all his troops and artillery from this side the river, and is on his way to join his worthy governor. Gholab Singh still remains faithful to us; but there is no knowing what side he will take, if things were to go at all against us. Called on the 31st. S——is laid up with fever; sat some time with him, and then returned to camp. Didn't go to dinner, but stayed and kept De M—— company.

Sunday, Nov. 12—My turn for duty. Up at daybreak, and relieved B——; marched off the guards—and here I am for the day, with my tent pitched right in front of the camp, next to the quarter-guard; and here I shall have to stay until I am relieved tomorrow morning. Rather lively work! with not a soul to speak to, except the men of my guard, with whom, of course, I can hold no intercourse except on duty. The 46th and 36th N. I. arrived this morning, and the 53rd Queen's are expected shortly; so we shall soon have a large force here. Stayed with my guard all day, went to mess in the evening, returned to my tent, and sat outside waiting for the captain to come round, which he did at eleven; turned out the guard, and made my report; then passed round the camp, and visited the sentries; walked about till twelve, then went into my tent, and wrote till about two; when I lay down with my clothes on, all ready to turn out if necessary, and went to sleep as well as the cold, which was piercing, would let me.

Nov. 13—Up at sunrise, waited till I was relieved, and returned to camp; went to see a cricket-match played between the horse and foot artillery; heard an account of the late affair at Mooltan read: it seems to have been a very sharp fight, and to have reflected great credit on our troops. A large body of General Courtlandt's Sikh force went over to the enemy just before, and something was necessary to rouse the spirits of the others. Nothing worth mentioning occurred in the day.

Nov. 14—Played cricket-match all day; awful hard work playing in the sun. At mess in the evening, we heard a great deal of firing from the other side of the river—probably some new force has joined the enemy, and they were giving them a salute. Walked about some time, and then went to bed. You've no idea what I suffer from the cold in the wretched hut I live in; it is open to the wind in all directions, and the air now is piercing cold. I lie and shiver in my bed, and can scarcely get any sleep: pretty work this campaigning for a delicately-nurtured youth like myself!

Nov. 15—Continued cricket-match—the officers of our corps against the officers of the camp: the first game that has ever been played in these wilds, I fancy, considering no Europeans have ever been here before. Came back to camp rather exhausted with my day's work; it's not like playing cricket in England this! Had a bathe and went to mess. We are to march tomorrow to dislodge some advanced troops of the enemy, who have crossed the river—and are very likely to have a scrimmage.

Nov. 16—Marched at four—bitter cold, the 2nd Europeans in front, and the six native corps bringing up the rear: the cavalry as usual on either flank, except the 3rd Dragoons, who acted as advanced guards with one troop of horse-artillery. About ten o'clock we heard guns ahead, though at some distance, and we all hoped that we were in for it; but no—it isn't in the nature of the brutes to stand; and when we arrived at our ground about twelve o'clock, after a most fatiguing march in the hot sun, we found all clear, and no enemy in sight. Pitched our camp, and got breakfast at one o'clock. I am rather unwell, from the effects of my exertions yesterday, and the sun today; but, by keeping quiet, hope to be all right in the evening. Not allowed to keep quiet, however. My poor horse was brought back, with a strong recommendation to me to shoot him, as he was in great pain: loaded my gun, and had him led about a quarter of a mile out of camp, when I put an end to the poor fellow's misery. His death was instantaneous, and I didn't stay to look at him, but returned to camp, feeling as if I had lost an old friend. General Campbell and his reconnoitring party were fired on today, from a small neighbouring fort, held by about five hundred of the enemy; why they are not dislodged I can't say. We have enough to lick thirty thousand of them.

Chapter 2

Battle of Ramnuggur

Nov. 16—By the bye, as you have a good map of India, I may as well give you an idea of our present position. Look out for Ramnuggur on the Chenab river, and then run along to the right, until you come to Wuzeerabad. We occupy a central position between the two, about ten miles on this side; and both places are held by the enemy, who keep up an incessant cannonading at vacancy—either, I believe, to get used to the sound, and to keep their pluck up, or else try and frighten us. Shere Singh expresses his determination to fight shortly; I hope he'll stick to his resolution. We have a beautiful view of the Cashmere range here. As brigade-subaltern of the day, I had to go and march off the rear picket at sunset; posted them about five hundred yards in rear of the regiment, and placed my sentries so as to establish a line of communication between us, and the other camps; ordered my tent out, and returned to dinner. At mess, from some report that the enemy intended an attack, three companies, Nos. 1, 2, and 3, were ordered out, to form an outlying picket in front of the camp; so I had to withdraw my men, and go with my company. Captain C——being ill, E——and myself had charge of it. Marched the men out, about five hundred yards, and then pitched our tents, and prepared to pass the night as pleasantly as possible, which was rather difficult, as after we had posted our sentries, and received our orders, every five minutes some staff-officer came galloping in, and we had to stand to our arms. At last, however, it grew quiet, and we retired to our tents, where we wrapped ourselves up as warm as possible, smoked our cheroots, and sat and talked. There was an incessant firing from Ramnuggur all night: we could see plainly the flash of each gun as it was discharged. What they were wasting their powder on, heaven only knows! About two, we lay down with our swords on, and slept till daybreak, though the cold was so intense that I awoke several times.

Nov. 17—Up at daybreak. Struck our tents, and marched back to the camp; joined the regiment, which was drawn up in front, under arms, and waiting for orders. After an hour and a half's shivering in the cold raw air, we were informed that the Sikhs had retired again, and that we were to return to camp, and re-pitch our tents. Breakfasted and wrote. Poor Deception is very ill; I'm almost afraid I shall lose him: misfortunes never come singly. Gave him some medicine, and then returned to my writing-desk, which is almost my sole occupation, when there is nothing exciting going on.

Nov. 18—The 61st Queen's came in this morning, and Wheeler's brigade is only a short distance off, so that we are no longer the only European infantry present.

Sunday, Nov. 19—Divine service in the mess tent: the first time we have been able to attend public worship for many months. The service was read by our commanding officer, and a very impressive sight it was. All the Protestants of the regiment were present, drawn up, standing round the walls of the tent, with the officers in the centre. There was something very solemn in the spectacle of so many gallant soldiers listening in respectful and devotional silence to the precepts of Christianity, and joining in the responses of our beautiful church service. Spent the day in my tent, went to mess, and retired early.

Nov. 21—The Commander-in-Chief has arrived at last, with a large accession of troops. Our army now consists of about fifteen thousand, of which there are about five thousand Europeans. Went to mess in the evening, and sat up rather late, when an aide-de-camp came in with an order to the brigadier, that we were to muster at three o'clock in perfect silence, and to march, leaving our camp standing, and one brigade to guard the camp. Consequently I turned in, to get a little sleep, as these silent movements looked very much like work.

Nov. 22—Paraded at three, and marched in total silence. Traversed about twelve miles across the country before daybreak, and drew up before a small fort where the enemy had lately been. The horse artillery were ordered on ahead, and, before five minutes had elapsed, we heard them hard at work, banging away like mad. Waited with great impatience for the order to advance, and the whole of the infantry moved forward in echelon of regiments. Passed the fort, and there, before us, on the other side of the river, lay the enemy's camp: we could see them plainly, and they appeared an immense army. Halted within range, piled arms, and watched the operations. Our artillery were hotly engaged with theirs, firing from opposite sides: and we, as we afterwards heard, had been ordered forward to effect a diversion in favour of the artillery—that is, to draw off the enemy's fire, (very obliging of the Chief!)—so we sat down and smoked our cheroots, and were fired at. However, all their shot was wide, and either went over us or to one side. One ball passed close over Lord Gough's head—rather a near shave—and killed two men out of the 61st on our right. One of our guns got fixed in a quicksand, and they were obliged to leave it to the enemy.

Presently a body of Sikhs crossed over, and commenced an annoying fire on our artillery. The 3rd and 14th Dragoons charged them, and drove them back, but with considerable loss. General Cureton was shot dead at the head of his regiment; Colonel Havelock likewise killed. Colonel Alexander lost an arm, and several of the officers received bad wounds. Fifty of the dragoons were killed or wounded; several artillerymen killed. The infantry suffered very slightly; not a man of ours touched. The fire at last got so hot that we were obliged to retire out of range. The enemy are on the other side of an un-fordable river, and in a very strong position, and we have no boats. General Cureton's death is a great loss; he was a splendid officer, much beloved, and a personal friend of the Chief's. Two of his sons are with the army. I saw him, poor fellow, just before his death; he was riding along in front of our regiment, when a round-shot passed close over his head.

Somebody remarked—"Rather a near shave that, general."—"Oh, I am used to it" replied he, smiling, and stroking his moustaches. In three minutes more, he was lying on the sand with a ball through his head, and many a brave fellow by his side. We are to wait for the arrival of our heavy guns and Thackwell's brigade. Bivouacked the whole day in the open air, without anything to eat, or put our heads under.

The enemy kept up an incessant firing all day, as if in derision of us, and we certainly have not done much good this time. I got my head underneath a saddle, and slept till sunset, when I had to go with my company on out-lying picket. Marched them off five hundred yards to the front, posted my sentinels, and lay down on the ground, until the dew falling, and the chilliness of my limbs, warning me of the danger of doing so, I got up and walked about, and by this means managed to keep myself warm. Drank off a glass of rum, and eat a piece of bread, which my sergeant brought me very kindly, and felt "pretty jolly under creditable circumstances." The enemy still kept up firing. I saw the bright flashes of the guns quite plainly; then came a rushing sound over my head through the air, and then the booming report followed. However we were protected by a rising ground, and none of the shot came near us. About eleven my tent came up; I pitched it, and, wrapping myself in a cloak, went to sleep—only awakened at intervals by the excessive cold.

We shall have a hard battle soon; and perhaps my fate may be that of many a brave fellow, who marched this morning full of life and daring, and now lies cold and motionless in the long sleep of death: if it should be so, my last thoughts were of you—my love remained unchanged unto the end. God bless you all! I trust, indeed, that the same Providence that has watched over me hitherto will protect me now, and we shall meet again; but, whatever happens, you shall hear of me as doing my part bravely as a soldier and a ———.

Nov. 23—Withdrew my picket at daybreak, and came into camp. Had my tent pitched, changed my clothes, and enjoyed the luxury of a wash, which I was not able to obtain yesterday. Got breakfast at nine, and you may imagine that we enjoyed it. We do not, I believe, do anything today, but are waiting for the arrival of our commissariat. The list of casualties, as far as we can ascertain, are—General Cureton, killed; Colonel Havelock, missing; Colonel Alexander, wounded; Captains Riley, Gaul, and Fitzgerald, with sword-cuts—the latter mortally; two officers, whose names I don't know, with spent balls; twenty-seven men killed, and twenty-three wounded out of the 14th Dragoons, and seven or eight in the 3rd Dragoons. The reason of the loss sustained by the 14th was, that in their charge they came on a deep *nullah* or ravine; the 3rd Dragoons pulled up; but the 14th—splendid, dashing fellows—they all charged through it; and, in the confusion into which they were thrown, they were fired into by the enemy, who chose their position with great tact—and a number of them knocked over. However they formed on the other side, charged, and drove the enemy into the river, a great number of whom were drowned in the crossing. Several other officers were wounded whose names are not yet known, and one or two of the artillery. The loss of the gun was a serious affair. Holmes of the 12th Irregulars was wounded—shot through the lungs, I hear, while lifting up the body of General Cureton. Stayed at home writing all morning, *tiffed*, and then put on my full dress to attend the funeral of General Cureton. Rode to the burying-ground; but, just as the procession arrived, there was an alarm, the drums beat to arms, and we had to gallop back to camp as quickly as possible. Dressed, and joined the regiment in front, where we were drawn up for half an hour, and then dismissed. Dined, and went to bed early, where I enjoyed a good night's sleep. We do not move, I believe, until Thursday, but are to wait for the arrival of some twenty-four-pounders.

Nov. 24—Breakfasted, and wandered about camp, doing nothing. One of our men was taken prisoner this morning. He wandered foolishly outside the pickets, and was carried off by one of the enemy's cavalry. Two sepoys also of the 21st were cut to pieces. Another sepoy was badly wounded, but managed to crawl into camp: his whole back is laid open, but he is likely to recover. Several of saw him, and say he is a fine brave fellow and bears his wounds splendidly. As the doctor was sewing them up, he asked for a little water, and while drinking, said—"Never mind me, Sahib; go on stitching." By the bye, I quite forgot to say that the 5th Light Cavalry behaved beautifully the day before yesterday; they have twenty-seven killed and wounded.

Evening.—Our *dak* from Lahore has been seized, and a lot of parcels. The enemy are in great feather, and ride along within half a mile of our camp, and close to our pickets. W—— of the 24th N. I. knocked over one with his rifle, the other day. He was strolling about, with a native blanket over his shoulders, outside the videttes, when a Sikh horseman, seeing what he thought an un-armed man, rode at him, and was going to cut him down, on which W—— quietly dropped his blanket, and shot him dead. Shere Singh wrote in this morning, to say, that if we will give him up Lahore, he will not molest us. He'll alter his tune before long. Major Lawrence, his wife, and child, have, I am sorry to say, been taken by Chuttur Singh. Attock is besieged by the same gentle-man, and bravely defended by Lieutenant Herbert, who is in charge of it with nineteen guns. The Chief, it is said, wishes to allow the two Singhs to effect a junc-tion, and take them in one fell swoop. Took a ride out in the evening to the observatory, and had a look at the enemy through a telescope; they are in great numbers on this side of the river, and seem to be very busy doing something. As for their guns, they give them no rest day or night—perpetual banging. They must have the maga-zines of the world at their disposal. Went to bed early.

Nov. 25—We are very busy now, throwing up batter-ies to commence operations. Two companies of our's are out today. The man of our regiment who was taken pris-oner yesterday was brought in this morning by four Sikhs, with "Shere Singh's compliments." He is such a perfect fool that they could get nothing out of him. No more can we;

though questioned by several of the staff, he could give no information whatever. He said that "the murthering thieves had tied him to a log, and put a guard over him;" but "sorra a bit did he get to ate or drink," and he was half-famished. He is a perfect Yahoo—just caught from the wilds of Ireland, and can speak very little English. He belongs to my company, to its credit; but as we only want hands, not heads, it's no matter. Went over in the afternoon to visit the batteries, and see how the work was getting on. They fired two guns at us, which came unpleasantly close, but did no damage. Took a short ride in the evening. General Wheeler has had a brush with the enemy a short distance off, and gave them a nice thrashing. The belief is, that if we don't gain a victory soon, Gholab Singh will join the Sikhs immediately, with all his force.

Sunday, Nov. 26—Breakfasted, and then had to go with my company to finish the work at one of the batteries. Completed it by twelve, and returned to camp. Attended divine service at four, performed by the army chaplain for our division. After that, I had to go and bury a poor fellow in my company who died last night. His grave was dug under a large tree, a short way from camp; and in it, after the solemn service had been performed, his body was laid. No coffin covered his remains: his bed-clothes disguised, though they could not hide, the rigid form of the corpse; and thus he was lowered in. Three volleys were fired over him, and all departed, except a few who stayed to see the work completed. I was much pleased with an action of theirs, which showed a great deal of feeling. Before the earth was thrown in, they brought a number of green boughs, and two of them descending, wove a sort of leafy canopy over him, to keep the earth from pressing too heavily on their unconscious comrade. How soon, I thought, may such a grave, or even a less ceremonious one, be mine; no friend or relative

45

will ever know the spot—none ever shed a tear over it. Far away from human habitation—no countryman may pass the place, until the name is obliterated by time.

One in the region of the East,
By a dark stream is laid,
The Indian knows his place of rest,
Deep in the cedar shade.

Went to mess in the evening, and after a short time retired to bed.

Nov. 27—Up at sunrise; paraded for the inspection of his Excellency the Commander-in-Chief. After a quarter of an hour's shivering under arms, his lordship with his staff behind him swept by. The colours were lowered, the band struck up, the men presented arms, the officers saluted—and on passed the glittering and prancing cavalcade, and we returned to our tents. Poor Fitzgerald died in the night: "poor fellow!" say all who hear of it, and he is forgotten. I am on duty today, and have, as usual, to pitch my tent by the guard, and remain there in lonely stupidity; but as tomorrow is the last day for the mail, I will spend my day in writing. Remained all day at my post; went to mess in the evening; dined, and then returned. The enemy were firing away at a fine rate, saluting the new moon. I hear General Steinbach, the leader of Gholab Singh's army, has had a brush with Chuttur Singh, who is on his way down, and given him the worst of it. Slept in my clothes all night; had to turn out three or four times to make my report to the different officers going round; but at last got to sleep.

Nov. 28—Returned at sunrise; wrote letters all day. The enemy are very busy mining on both banks of the river: we can see them plainly through a glass. We are waiting the arrival of our heavy guns to commence the attack—it will be a hard piece of fighting, if they only remain firm. Colonel Havelock has never been heard of, and there is but little doubt of his fate; he was seen wounded and surrounded by the enemy. Holmes is doing well; he is a splendid fellow, and brave as a lion: he was shot while carrying off General Cureton's body alone from under a heavy fire. Received your last letter today, and my uncle's; paraded in the afternoon, and in the evening had to go out with my company on picket; passed the night under arms, as the Chief expected an attack; however, all was quiet. And now I must conclude for the present. Before this reaches you, there will have been an engagement. With my tenderest love to all, good-by.

CHAPTER 3

Crossing the Chenab

Nov. 29—Marched in my picket at daybreak; dressed; walked about till breakfast-time; and then, having devoured my morning meal, sat down to complete my overland despatch. Upon my life, I pity you, if you ever get it, and have to read it through: I did so myself, and I assure you it was very hard work, and I only got the packet finished just in time. Felt in father low spirits after I had sent it off; so took a walk over to the artillery, to freshen myself. Joined a lot of fellows at B——'s tent, and discussed very learnedly the best mode of attack; sat there chatting until sunset, and then returned to camp. Took a *mussack* of cold water, very cold—capital thing for the health; went to mess; dined, and sat some time discussing our present circumstances. The enemy are strongly entrenched—the bank on both sides probably well mined; and their guns so well masked that it would take our artillery a good two hours to dislodge them at such a distance as eight hundred yards. But enough—we shall see what we shall see.

Nov. 30—Paraded at sunrise for exercise; had a couple of hours of it; breakfasted, and here I am. Stayed in camp all day writing. We are to attack tomorrow. Campbell's division has moved off to the right about nine miles, to cross at a ford, and take the enemy in flank; we attack, I believe, in front. The heavy guns have arrived, and a lot of our men are out tonight constructing a battery for them. Went to mess, and spent a very pleasant evening. About nine a vidette came galloping in, to say that the enemy were advancing; got all ready; but it turned out to be a false alarm. Walked out, and visited the picket; had a chat with T——, and then came back and went to bed.

Dec. 1—We attack today, I believe at one, as soon as General Campbell has got to his place—and then for my first action. Breakfasted at eight, and here I am writing: if I ever finish this page, I hope to have something worth recording.

Evening.—At nine o'clock the right wing was ordered out to work at the throwing up of a new battery in front of the one we raised the other day, and about three hundred yards in advance; the left wing had been working at it all night, and we relieved them. Heard, that from Sir Joseph Thackwell's and Campbell's divisions being opposed at the place where they were intended to have crossed, they had gone on to Wuzeerabad, and therefore the attack could not take place that day. Worked away until four o'clock, when we finished the battery: it consists of two 24-pounders, three mortars, and four eight-inch howitzers. There is another battery thrown up on the left of this. They say we shall attack for certain tomorrow morning. Spent a very pleasant evening at mess; had an argument with several of our's in defence of Sir Walter Scott's poems, which they had the bad taste to pronounce second-rate—you've no idea how one enjoys a quiet dinner and a comfortable chat, after being out all day in the sun. Turned in about ten, and slept like a top.

Dec. 2—Breakfasted at eight; some unforeseen delay has detained Sir J. Thackwell, and we don't attack today after all. Out at nine with the right wing, to act as a covering party to the artillery. The Chief came up at ten, and, after reconnoitring for some time, would stand it no longer, and ordered the batteries to open on the enemy. They commenced an uproar such as I never heard before; the twenty-fours went off with a roar that shook the very earth; and the shot rushed through the air with a noise like a mighty winged spirit, till the very atmosphere was stunned. I was looking through a telescope all the time, and saw where each shot took effect. The enemy were all in their trenches in five minutes, the tents struck, and not a man to be seen; some of the shells were beautifully pitched, and burst right above them—they must have done great execution. Presently they opened on us with their batteries, and kept up a sharp cannonading all day: however, we were so well protected that only one man was knocked over, losing his leg just below the knee; an ammunition-wagon was blown up by one of the shells, and exploded with an awful row, but, wonderful to say, not a soul was hurt. We continued out all day, during which time the firing was kept up; we were then relieved and marched into camp. Dined, sat a short time, and went to bed, as I have to go out again with a working party at one o'clock.

Dec. 3—Up at one, and dressed. Joined the right wing in front, and marched off for the new battery. Somehow or other, in the dark, we managed to lose our way, and, after two hours' walking about, found ourselves on the banks of the river, and so close that we could hear the enemy talking and working. Crept back again in total silence, expecting to be opened on every minute, and at last managed to reach camp, whence we started again, and, after a good deal of trouble, and walking at least six miles, found out our party, who were throwing up a breastwork within 150 yards of the river; relieved them, and worked away in total silence until daybreak, when we had finished, and had constructed two batteries, and a breastwork of 300 yards at least, with a deep ditch for infantry. At daybreak we expected their batteries would have opened upon us; but all was quiet, and not a man to be seen on the other side of the river. They have evidently withdrawn all their guns to oppose Campbell. At eight o'clock we were marched back again, and had just time to change our clothes, and take a hasty breakfast, when the whole brigade was ordered to march and join Campbell. Started at ten, and marched along the river to the right. The sun was fearfully hot, and the men were so knocked up with night-work, that it was quite painful to see their haggard appearance: they haven't had their accoutrements off for two days. I had got no horse, so I had to trudge along too, as well as I could; and hard work it was, I can tell you. After having walked about all night, reached the river at four o'clock, and halted while the boats were got ready. From two o'clock until evening we heard a heavy cannonading on the other side of the river—Thackwell and Campbell evidently hard at work. We were half mad at the idea that there was an action going on and we should be too late. We could see plainly immense clouds of smoke and dust rolling along on the other side; and, though we worked like horses, the boats were not ready until five. All the officers were up to their waists in water until seven o'clock, keeping the men back from crowding into the boats; and such a scene of shouting, struggling, and confusion, you never saw. It was all we could do, to restrain the men from overloading the boats; but at last we succeeded in crossing the whole regiment over: the 70th and 45th, however, were unable to cross that night. Drew up on the other side; piled arms, and prepared to bivouac for the night in our wet clothes. One man in my company managed to lose his shoes and unmentionables; so I, in the softness of my heart, lent him my cloak, and spent the night as well as I could, which, without covering, food, or fire, was miserably enough. I was obliged to walk about until my clothes dried—and then lay down on the damp ground, and slept at intervals of a quarter of an hour; varying the amusement by starting up and rushing furiously up and down, until I got into a glow; then lying down again, until the cold obliged me to repeat the process. And thus we passed the night, all of us most excessively miserable; and never, I believe, was dawn of day more welcomed than that which broke on. . . .

Dec. 4—By nine o'clock all the troops were crossed over, and, after devouring, like so many cannibals, some fragments of bread and cold meat, which made their appearance about eight o'clock, we resumed our march. Major Tait, with the 3rd Irregulars, joined us from the main body, and gave us an account of yesterday's proceedings. About two o'clock the enemy opened their fire on Campbell's division, which our artillery returned with interest, doing great execution; and this continued all day. The Chief having given orders not to advance, the infantry were not engaged; so we have lost nothing by not being up. The game at long bowls continued all afternoon: our loss was trifling; but the enemy suffered very severely. Lall Singh, one of their bravest sirdars, is reported killed; and in the night—would you credit it—they left their entrenched position; and when we joined the army, they were in full retreat toward the Jhelum, leaving their defences at Ramnuggur, which, as we have since discovered, we could not have taken without immense loss. They were enormously strong; entrenchments six deep; and their magazines so constructed as to be entirely bomb-proof. The river in front was breast-high, and very swift; so the Chief may congratulate himself on having gained possession so cheaply. However, the enemy suffered a good deal; some four hundred were lying dead on the ground as we passed; horses and men strewed about in heaps: it was my first view of the horrors of war, and a very sickening sight it was. Our troops suffered greatly from fatigue and hunger. The sepoys have not tasted food for two days; and the Europeans are almost as badly off. An officer's charger was shot dead, close to the 61st Queen's, and, before half an hour was passed, they had roasted him, dismembered him, and eaten him: rather delicate feeding, you will say. Well! to cut a long story short, we marched the whole day without food. The Chief crossed over at Ramnuggur and joined us, and we followed as fast as we could on the enemy's retreat; but with tired men and horses it was cruel work; and after twenty miles it was mere crawling along. However, we went toiling along until nine o'clock at night; officers and men equally done up; and then we halted, and, after devouring half a loaf of bread each, lay down by our arms, and passed another night on the bare ground, saturated with dew, and half frozen. I awoke two or three times in the night, and so great was the universal fatigue, that, from the large army assembled there, not a sound was heard. I could have fancied myself alone on the vast plain: at last, in spite of cold and everything else, I fell asleep, and slept till morning.

Dec. 5—Up at daybreak; picked some bones, and walked about until ten o'clock, when, to our great delight, our tents made their appearance. Pitched them as quickly as possible; luxuriated in a *mussack* of water, and a change of linen; and then, throwing myself on my bed, enjoyed a most refreshing sleep. I have got no bad effects from the last two days' bivouacking but a return of my old cough, which I have regularly every winter. Got dinner at half-past four; and thirty more hungry men, I'll venture to say, never sat down to table. We halt here, I believe, for some time. The enemy are about fifteen miles ahead; they have been augmented by the Peshawar troops, who, it was reported, had joined before under Chuttur Singh; but such was not the case. I suppose we shall be at them soon.

Dec. 6—Here we are still, all comfortable but awfully disgusted. We have gained a strong position, but we have lost the enemy; and when we shall catch them again, heaven only knows. The artillery lost between twenty and thirty men killed and wounded, and several officers. Our men have suffered a good deal from the cold and exposure; several have lost the use of their limbs, and one poor fellow is dying. They say that, after we have taught these fellows a lesson, the Punjab is to be abandoned, and that now we are to go back to Wuzeerabad until we hear of the fall of Mooltan, and to try and entice the Sikhs to advance again. Where they are at present, we cannot touch them: they have taken up their quarters in a large forest on the Jhelum, where cavalry and artillery are useless. Wrote most part of the morning; *tiffed*, and then played a game at cricket.

Dec. 8—Paraded for the inspection of the Chief. Had to wait the usual time in the cold. At last he came,—called out the major, and commended us highly for our steadiness on the 22nd, and our spirited exertions since—and kindly gave us credit for qualities which we have hardly had an opportunity to prove; although, I have no doubt, we should have been all he called us. However, we shall have a chance yet. After breakfast it came on to rain, and poured in torrents all morning. In the afternoon, it cleared up a little, and we changed ground for about two miles. In the evening, it came on again—the whole country was flooded, and we had literally to wade over to the mess-tent. In the middle of dinner, R——, whom I knew very well at Benares, and who has exchanged out of the 48th N.I., into our corps, arrived: he had ridden all the way from Ramnuggur in the rain, and was wet through. Brought him in, and gave him food, and something to keep off the bad effects of his ducking, and put him into my bed for the night, while I went and slept on the floor in B——'s tent—and a very pleasant time I had of it—with about six dogs tumbling over me all night—walking over my face—lying on my chest—and other amusing gambols.

Dec. 9—Up at daybreak, dressed, wandered about through the camp, which presented very much the appearance of the bed of a river just drained off. Breakfasted; presented R—— to the commanding officer—played cricket all day, and leap-frog by moonlight.

Sunday, Dec. 10—Stayed at home all day; sent my letter of introduction to Major Tait: I have had it in my desk for two years now, and never hoped to have an opportunity of delivering it. However, here he is, with his corps pitched close to us: a very fine set of fellows they are. I never should guess Major Tait to be a brother of the Doctor's—there is not the slightest resemblance either in voice or feature—though I doubt not there is in character, as Major Tait is universally liked.

Dec. 11—Up early, and took a ride on B——'s mare before breakfast. I am sorry to say Deception is so reduced with the influenza, and his recovery so extremely doubtful, that I have been obliged to part with him for about a quarter of his value originally; and now I am without a horse, and if I ever have another that's worth a song. . . . well, never mind! Breakfasted, wrote in the morning, and read a book on natural history which I managed to get hold of—played a game of cricket in the afternoon—bathed, and went to mess.

55

Dec. 12—All quiet. We don't know what we are going to do. We changed our encamping ground this afternoon, and are now in front of the whole army, at the commencement of a thick thorn jungle.

Dec. 13—Up early, and went out coursing in the jungle in front. Saw nothing but a reconnoitring party of the enemy, which, as we were only three in number, and unarmed, checked our further progress. Returned to breakfast. There are a great many rumours about at present, and it is doubtful whether they will not make some rotten treaty after all. Major Lawrence is a prisoner in the enemy's camp, and a good deal of negotiating is going on.

Dec. 14—Took a walk in a garden about two miles off, where we amused ourselves with eating oranges, and pelting one another with citrons and pomegranates, which hung on the trees in clusters. Spent an hour there wandering about very pleasantly, and then raced back to camp. I don't think I shall ever keep a horse again, as I can almost always get a mount from somebody—a friend's horse and my own spurs, shall be my maxim. Played quoits—took my daily bathe—dined at the artillery mess. Met Sir Richmond Shakespeare, who commands the battery nearest us: he was knighted for rescuing some ladies in Kabul, and seems a very intelligent man. He has travelled a great deal in Russia—and some of his stories were very amusing and instructive.

Sunday, Dec. 17—Service in the mess tent. At home all day. I don't know what we are to do next. Rather an odd state of things, with the enemy within twelve miles; but I believe we are waiting for the fall of Mooltan.

Dec. 18—We were ordered to march tomorrow, but the order was countermanded. In the middle of the night, we had a most tremendous storm—the thunder literally shook the ground, and the rain came down in torrents, dripping through my miserable tent, and wetting me to the skin. Spent a very pleasant evening in consequence.

Dec. 19—Bitterly cold after the rain—a cutting wind blowing all day. Wrote, wandered about, and was very miserable.

Dec. 21—Another cricket-match; nothing but cricket now-a-days. The enemy carried off 200 of our camels today out grazing. As it chanced, I saw a poor old villager brought in, shot through the head. The ball had passed through his temples, and his long grey hair was dabbled with blood, which trickled through the bottom of the bier, leaving a crimson trail along the ground. A few months ago, the sight would have sickened me; but I have seen so many such lately, that the feelings grow callous, and a passing sensation of oppression and pity was all the emotion it excited.

Dec. 23—At the quarter-guard on duty: wrote letters, and indulged in melancholy retrospections.

Sunday, Dec. 24—Service in the morning. Received your last, dear, over-land. . . . read it, and wrote all day. Took a meditative walk towards sunset, and thought of past Christmas days; returned, and wrote again till mess-time. Retired early.

Dec. 25—It is Christmas day. No merry bells are pealing their glad notes through the air—no green boughs adorn our desolate-looking camp. There is a forced cheerfulness on every brow, hiding the achings of a sad heart. They are thinking of the Christmas days passed by, poor fellows! and the contrast with the present seems to mock them. At a season like this, my heart yearns towards you. How vividly and how brightly fond memory calls up the past—how sweetly sound the voices of years gone by! God bless you all! A merry, merry Christmas to you, and a new year radiant with happiness. *Bang* go the big guns!—they are firing a salute in honour of the good old time. Merrily bubbles the old tin pot, in which the men, poor fellows! are boiling a round ball of mysterious compounds, which, in the innocence of their hearts, they call a plum-pudding—(the confounded thing was hissing away all last night)—and very proud they seem of their performance. "Reminds you of Christmas at home, this, sir", said one of them to me. "Oh! very much so, indeed," said I. But this is no day for re-pinings—let me at least keep up a semblance of old times, and not insult the spirit of the day by a clouded brow.

Hope has not ceased in my bosom to dwell,
And with radiant finger it beckons me on.

Up at sunrise, and took a walk; distributed a few merry Christmases to various disconsolate-looking individuals; attended Divine service. Partook of the Christmas dinner, and spent as merry an evening as we could, with the help of a few songs, and a skirl on the bagpipes, which drew all the Scotchmen in the regiment round the mess-tent.

Dec. 26—The Bombay troops have at last arrived at Mooltan, and operations were to have commenced today.

Dec. 27—Up at daybreak, and rode over to Ramnuggur with Sprot and De M——, to the Chiefs camp. One-third of the army is behind at Ramnuggur with the headquarters, on this side of the river, about six miles off.

Dec. 28, 1848—Camp, Keila. Thus ends the journal for the present. I am sorry I have no tale of battle to tell:

we have had lots of hard work, and some danger, but no general action. The affair of the 3rd was a brilliant thing for the artillery; but the infantry and cavalry had nothing to do. Where we shall be when you receive this, I don't know. Mooltan will probably have fallen, and a blow have been struck towards the destruction of those 40,000 gentlemen who have taken up their quarters in such near proximity to the army of the Punjab. And now, farewell. I trust that, in the next despatch, I shall have a tale to tell. Give my best love to all at home, and wish them for me a merry Christmas, and a Happy New Year! Do not be uneasy about me; I am under the protection of Him who ordereth all for the best.

CHAPTER 4

Battle of Chilianwalla

Dec. 29—Up at daybreak, and visited the provisions; relieved guard, breakfasted, played a game at cricket, wrote letters, went to mess, &c.

Dec. 30—Up early, marched off my guard; went down to the 70th, and found a lot of fellows practising leaping. Of course, I couldn't resist the opportunity; leapt up to my lip on level ground; can H—— or C—— beat that now? Had a foot-race afterwards, and lost it by a little—I suppose from being out of practice.

Dec. 31.—Marched to church parade in the afternoon with the regiment. The service was performed by Mr Whiting, the army chaplain, in front of the camp, where all the European troops were drawn up in a square. After it was over we marched back again, with our band playing. Sat up till twelve, to see the new year come in.

And here I am, after all the perils with which your fancy has doubtless pictured me as surrounded, safe and sound as ever, and about as ignorant of what will be the result of the campaign as when I last wrote. Lord Gough won't let me into his confidence, and I'm afraid I shan't be knighted this time. However, the Duke of Wellington didn't come out very strong in his first campaign, so there is some hope for me yet. Still, often do I long for the expiration of the years that must transpire before I again set foot in old England: what a time it seems! But it will pass quickly with me—shifting and changing, marching, novelty, and all that, make short work of the months that seem to crawl to you, poor stationary individuals. One thing I thank God for—I still keep my health, and am never sick or sorry. It is a great blessing out here, and I cannot be sufficiently thankful for it. I think the way I have been living this campaign would have killed most people—exposed to heat, cold, damp, and every description of discomfort—with a piece of rag stuck on the top of three poles, called a tent, to cover me, open to every quarter of the heaven, and through the top of which I nightly study astronomy. And yet, instead of being laid up with rheumatism, or prostrated with fever, I am in better health than most people in camp, and care no more for discomforts, than if I were as accustomed to exposure as a battery-horse, which is about the worst-treated animal I know. All this I attribute to having a good constitution, and not having been made a molly-coddle of at home.

Jan. 1, 1849—A Happy New Year to you! Awoke at day-break, by the band playing "The Light of other Days " at my tent. Very much obliged to them for the compliment, but wished them at the time anywhere else. Got up, however, and dressed. This is the commencement of a new year, the third new-year's day away from home. If three years ago I had looked forward, and seen where I was to spend this, I should have been considerably astonished. Here I am, pitched in the midst of a howling wilderness, with a sea of tents around me. If I go out to play a game at cricket, and hit a good swipe to *point*, the *field* has to fish the ball out from among the wheels of a battery; if I hit to *leg*, it goes slap into a stand of arms; and if to *long-slip*, it goes in amongst the sepoys' pots and pans, and probably destroys some poor devil's dinner. That's what you call cricket under novel circumstances! However, this is only our practice-ground; for matches, we have a piece of ground about a mile in the rear.

The Chief has moved his camp up from Ramnuggur to within three miles. A small body of troops has been sent off on a scour, to intercept a Sikh chief who is on his way, with some cavalry and two guns, to join Shere Singh. Whether they will succeed or not is doubtful.

Jan. 2—Rode over to the Chiefs camp, to play a cricket-match. The same every day.

Jan. 5—The suburbs of Mooltan have fallen—the work of destruction has begun; and while I write, many, whose fond relatives are anxiously waiting for the next letter from a son, a brother, or a husband, are lying in that voiceless sleep from which no sound shall wake them; and the next letter these fond ones will receive will bear the news of death on its sable borders. One of the enemy's magazines was blown up by a shell from our mortars, and an immense breach formed by the explosion. The Sikhs immediately after sprang up on the battlements, and fired a salvo from every gun on us. They are all brave fellows in that devoted garrison, and many a regiment will lose the number of its mess before the proud standard of England waves over its walls. They will have attacked by this time, and all is probably over. The loss at present is rather heavy: fifty-four killed and wounded, of whom eighteen are of-ficers—names as yet unknown. Playfair and Gordon of the 60th Rifles, killed, we know of. They say in the Chiefs camp that we shall be at long bowls again before next week is over.

Jan. 7—News from Mooltan—the city has fallen. The attack was made at two breaches at the same time. The 1st Bombay Fusileers, a sister corps, were the first to plant the standard on the walls. The other breach was found impracticable. So we have taken the shine out of the Queen's this time. Paraded for church service in the afternoon. We were all ordered to be on the alert in the morning, on account of large bodies of the enemy having been seen in front. Had to wait half-an-hour for the clergyman, who did not come after all, and the service was read by the brigadier.

Jan. 8—At dinner there was an alarm, and my company was ordered out; so we had to leave the untasted viands, and sally forth. . . . The alarm proved, as usual, to be a false one, and originated in a small party of cavalry, who were escorting provisions from a neighbouring village, having been attacked by two hundred of the Sikhs, and one of them cut down. The rest galloped in and gave the alarm to our pickets, who spread it to the camp.

Jan. 9—Marched at eight o'clock to change ground to our right front, our brigade as rearguard. I never saw anything like the filth of the camp; it certainly was a necessary movement: dead camels, bullocks, and *tattoes* lying about in all directions, all raw and half-devoured by the jackals and vultures, who hardly took any notice of us as we passed. Several camels fell down on the march, and were left to die. The niggers have a prejudice against taking away any life, except that of a human being; and if a poor brute is unable to proceed, from lameness, weakness, or any other cause, he is left, where he falls, to linger out his last agonies, and perish by a death of starvation at last. Went out with my company on picket at sunset, five hundred yards in front, posted the sentries so as to communicate with the cavalry on our right, and the 70th on our left, and then lay down in our clothes. There are three of us with the company, N—— in command. Passed the night without being disturbed by anyone except Jack Frost, who is in great force now.

Jan. 10—Marched in with the picket. Parade for inspection of General Gilbert at half-past four.

Jan. 11—Paraded for the inspection of the Chief, who told us we were to attack tomorrow. Played a cricket-match against the artillery. God bless you all, and preserve me in the hour of battle to embrace you again!

Jan. 12—Marched at seven o'clock, and got up to the place on the borders of the jungle where the enemy were; but they had retired to their defences; and when we reached our ground about two o'clock, after a most fatiguing march, they had all decamped. We pitched our camp for the day, dressed, and went to dinner. We attack without doubt tomorrow. Spent a very happy evening, and retired about twelve, after shaking hands with one another.

Jan. 14—Two days have passed over, and, thank God I am here to tell you. We have had as severe an action as ever was fought in India. But I will go back, and give it you all in detail.

On the morning of the 13th we marched at seven, struck our tents, took a glass of wine all together, and drank to every man's safety in the approaching action. Marched about ten miles, and came upon a thick jungle, where we were halted about an hour. The artillery went ahead—and presently we heard the cannonading commence—*bang, bang* went the guns, one after the other, in one continued, stunning roar; and our hearts beat, and our pulses quickened with anticipation. The enemy took it up, and a tremendous fire was kept up for about half-an-hour, when the word came for the infantry to advance—"Fix bayonets! Load! Deploy into line! Quick march!" And just then came a roll of musketry, that drove us almost to madness. "Quick march!" And into the jungle we plunged in line with a deafening cheer, the roll of musketry increasing every moment.

On we went at a rapid double—dashing through the bushes, and bounding over every impediment; faster rolled the musketry—crash upon crash the cannon poured forth its deadly contents. On swept our brigade, and, gaining an open space in the jungle, the whole of the enemy's line burst on our view. "Charge!" rang the word through our ranks, and the men bounded forward like angry bull-dogs, pouring in a murderous fire. The enemy's bullets whizzed above our heads; the very air seemed teeming with them; man after man was struck down, and rolled in the dust. But a passing glance was all we could give them. And onward we went, bearing on their line with a steadiness which nothing could resist. They fired a last volley, wavered, and then turned and fled, leaving the ground covered with dead and wounded.

Pursuit in a jungle like that was useless, where we could not see twenty yards before us; so we halted, and began to collect our wounded—when all of a sudden a fire was opened upon us in our rear. A large body of the enemy had turned our flank in jungle, and got between us and the rest of our troops; another party were on our left and we found ourselves, with one light field-canon completely surrounded and alone in the jungle. The word was given, " Right-about face", and we advanced steadily, loading and firing as we went. Captain Dawes' battery was then behind us. As the cavalry were bearing down the brigadier shouted, "A shower of guns there!" and every gun was turned on, the men working as coolly as on parade, a salvo was poured in, that sent horses and men head over heels, in heaps. If it had not been for that battery, we should have been cut down to a man.

The fire was fearful; the atmosphere seemed alive with balls: I can only compare it to a storm of hail. They sang above my head and ears so thick, that I felt that if I put out my hand, it would be taken off. A man was knocked over on either side of me, and I expected every moment to be hit, so incessant was the storm of balls. I thought about you all, and breathed a short prayer—it was all I had time for, for we were obliged to be almost everywhere at once, keeping the men in line, which, from the jungle, was extremely difficult. Our firing was beautiful: every man was as steady as a rock, and fired low and well; while the sepoys on our right were blazing away into the air, and taking no aim whatever.

All this time the enemy were dodging about the bushes, banging away at us, and then disappearing. At last General Gilbert rode up, and said to Steel, "Well, major, how are you? Do you think you are near enough to charge?"

"By all means," said Steel.

"Well, then, let's see how you can do it."

"Men of the 2nd Europeans, prepare to charge—Charge!"

And on we went with a stunning cheer. Poor Nightingale was shot in the head, and fell at my feet. I had just time to order two men to pick him up. The Sikhs fought like devils. They charged down on us, singly, sword in hand, and strove to break through our line. But it was no go; and after a short struggle we swept them before us, and remained masters of the field. This is only what happened in our part of the field. The battle was general all over the line, and we were in the extreme right, and the thickness of the jungle prevented our seeing what was going on anywhere else. We took three of their guns in our second charge, and spiked them on the ground. After all was over, we did what we could for our wounded—and a fearful sight it was, and one to make a man's heart bleed: poor fellows lying on the ground and writhing in agony, and not a doctor or drop of water to be got.

One poor fellow in my company was mortally wounded in the stomach, and lay bleeding to death; another had his leg struck off, and the quivering of his frame was fearful. The enemy lay in heaps around—some dead, some dying—but fierce and untamed even in their dying struggle: numbers of them were bayoneted by our men in the act of rearing themselves up, and taking aim at the officers. Several of our wounded were cut to pieces in the rear, where we had been obliged to leave them in the charge. Surrounded as we were, it couldn't be avoided, and fearful was the retaliation the Europeans took for it—not a man was spared. The battle lasted for three hours; and so maddening was the excitement that it seemed scarcely half-an-hour.

The Chief rode down our line afterwards: we gave him three cheers; and proud we were of the praise he gave us. In short, we have gained ourselves a name. The brigadier and major did all that commanding officers could do. The colours were carried gallantly by De Mole and Toogood, the two senior ensigns, and are shot through and through. Our own loss is about seventy killed and wounded; and our not having lost more may be attributed to the beautiful order we kept, and the admirable way in which we were supported by Captain Dawes' battery.

But alas! in other parts of the field, the loss has been tremendous. The 24th Queen's charged up to a battery, and just as they gained the muzzles of the guns, exhausted and out of breath, grape was poured into them, and they were driven back in confusion, leaving 450 of their men on the ground. The 56th N. I. suffered dreadfully too, and lost their colours: four guns of Captain Christie's troop were taken by the enemy; Christie killed. The enemy were 60,000 all arms—which was fearful odds. They overlapped us in numbers on each flank. Such a mass of men I never set eyes on, and as plucky as lions: they ran right on the bayonets of the 24th, and struck at their assailants when they were transfixed. Men who have seen many a campaign, say it was the ugliest piece of fighting they ever had anything to do with—a general action in a jungle, where you couldn't see twenty yards, and were pelted at from every bush. My leaping powers were in great requisition, and saved me many a scratch.

Everyone fought as if the blood of kings was in his veins, and each man emulated his fellow. If we had only had two more hours of daylight, we should have taken every gun they had, and smashed them altogether; but, even as it is, their loss must have been tremendous. In front of our regiment they lay in heaps of thirties and forties; and in other parts of the line, where our artillery was thicker, the carnage was immense. I had two or three very narrow escapes; a man's arm was taken away with a round-shot, touching me; I had one shoulder-knot shot off; and a fellow who was lying with a leg smashed, about ten yards in front, was taking a steady aim at me, when I rushed forward to disarm him. He fired, and the ball whizzed past my ear; I tried to save him, but before I could interpose, he was riddled with bayonets, and so, I am sorry to say, were almost all the wounded. There is no holding in the men when their blood is up.

Our loss was somewhere on three thousand killed and wounded; and the slaughter amongst the officers is very great. Thirteen officers of the 24th Queen's alone are lying dead in one tent, and three more are dying. Nightingale's wound is very dangerous; the ball went in over the eye, and traversed round the skull. But I am sick of the details of slaughter; our victory is dearly purchased.

At sunset we collected as many of our wounded as we could find, blew up all the ammunition that we had taken, and moved out of the jungle into the open ground, where we piled arms and bivouacked on the ground. A more wretched night I never passed: it came on a thick drizzling rain, and we were wet to the skin—to sleep was impossible, and we were almost perishing with thirst. In my wanderings about in search of water, I came upon the field hospital, and the sight I saw there I shall remember to my dying day—poor wounded wretches lying on the ground without a thing to cover them. "Water—water—water! " was their ceaseless cry, and not a drop was there to slake their thirst. All the hospital apparatus was behind, and there was not a single comfort for the poor fellows: even medical assistance was very scarce; many were lying bleeding on the cold earth for hours, without having a soul near them. The ghastly sight of suffering, the fearful wounds and hideous gashes that met my eyes, would poison an angel's dreams. Never was dawn—a miserable and a rainy one as it was—so welcome.

Jan. 14—At daybreak the ground was marked out for an encampment, and we moved up in order. A mounted officer was sent off for the baggage, and we kept ourselves warm by walking about. The Chief then rode all along the line, and congratulated us on our success. We gave him three enthusiastic cheers—caps flew up in the clouds—and the fine old fellow, with his grey hairs uncovered to the rain, passed on along the troops, speaking kindly to all, and one wild ringing cheer went down from one end to the other. At eleven o'clock our tent came up, and we got something to drink, and, throwing off our wet clothes, turned into bed; and in spite of the storm of rain and wind which lasted through the whole day with great violence, slept like tops till dinnertime, when we had the first food we had tasted for two days. And didn't we just enjoy it? Put my bed into Sprot's tent for the night, as my own was leaking like a sieve.

Jan. 15—A miserable, wretched day—the rain pouring down in torrents. Visited our sick men in hospital, and spoke to the poor fellows. They are doing as well as can be expected, and great hopes are entertained of poor Nightingale. We brought in, I am sorry to say, only about twenty of the guns we took; the enemy, I fear, have recovered the rest: however, they'll have some work to unspike them. Mooltan, is reported to have fallen, and they say we are to follow up our advantages directly. The Sikhs, though they have received a smashing, are by no means done for yet,—and, from the way in which we have suffered, it is a very ticklish business. Confound this jungle work. Oh! for one day at the scoundrels in the open. At four o'clock I went with the rest of the officers to the funeral—a melancholy office it was. The heavens were black with clouds, and the rain poured down incessantly. Twenty-five officers were buried in one spot; thirteen of the 24th Queen's were brought up one after another, and buried in one grave. Brigadier Pennycuick and his son were buried in another. The father was cut down first; and his son threw himself on his body, and was killed there. Major Christie was buried in the same grave with his men; they fell together—and now they sleep together in the bed of glory. Ekins, the Deputy-Adjutant-General, was buried there also. The enemy, we hear, have not crossed the river, but are about four

miles ahead. Waded over to mess, where a most miserable attempt at dinner awaited us. The servants are unable to light a fire sufficient to cook with, and consequently everything was raw: however, we were thankful to have whole throats to eat with. The rain continued all night, and my bed-clothes were wet through; but it did not hinder me from sleeping soundly till morning.

Jan. 16—Still raining—wretched, wretched weather, and very disheartening to the troops. Went to the hospital—the men are most of them doing as well as can be expected. One poor fellow in my company, who was shot close to me, died in the night. Nightingale is in a dangerous state, but hopes are held out of him. Young Godby is severely wounded, and young Cureton killed. They say we are to wait here for reinforcements; and indeed it is necessary, for we are awfully crippled. At four o'clock we buried poor Walden. The clergyman was unable to attend, so I had to read the service over him: the rain was pouring all the time, and as there was no gravedigger present, the men had to fill in the grave with their hands and bayonets. The enemy's tents are plainly to be seen on a hill about four miles off. A sepoy, who had been taken prisoner, was sent back this morning with a message from Shere Singh. He says that the enemy's wounded are lying in heaps on the hill without any attendance—left to die of their wounds.

Jan. 17—A beautiful day, thank God! The bright sunshine has come out again; and no one who has not experienced the misery of wading through a wet camp, with mud up to the ankles, can appreciate the blessing dry weather is to a campaigner. Rode out to see the battle-field—a sickening sight it was. The enemy had come down in the night, after we left the ground, and murdered every wounded man. Many of them had evidently only been hit in the legs, and they were gashed about in a fearful manner. Every man had his throat cut, and many their heads clean cut off. One poor man of ours was obliged to be left behind in the charge, and a lot of the enemy came down and literally hewed him in pieces. Another, who is now lying, doing well, in the hospital, was awfully cut about too. He says that they took him and tossed him up in the air, to see if he was alive; but, as he himself quaintly expressed it, "he had the presence of mind to be dead".

The most fearful sight of all was in front of the battery where the 24th had been repulsed. One hundred and fifty of them lay dead on the ground. They were literally in heaps. The hideous way they had been mangled by these inhuman fiends no tongue can describe; and no mercy will be shown by our infuriated soldiers to any who fall in their way. There were immense heaps of Sikhs lying there too, but they had taken away the greater number. They fired a salute of twenty-one guns this morning, to commemorate the arrival of some new rebel gentleman with a large force. Five companies had to go out as a working party—we are, "'tis true, pity 'tis, 'tis true," entrenching ourselves—that looks very much like waiting for the arrival of the Mooltan troops. Europeans we want; without more European infantry we can do nothing. Worked away at the breastwork until seven o'clock, when we were relieved. All this style of thing falls upon the Europeans, as the sepoys have a prejudice against it—no fools they, for that same. However, I was glad to see them clearing away the jungle in front.

Jan. 18—Played a game at cricket; it has become a sort of monomania with me. You remember how fond I was of it at home; I am twice as much so now. At four o'clock, I went out with my company to the front, to protect the working party—a very pleasant duty to be ordered on suddenly, as it entails the necessity of going out supperless and tentless, and passing a night *sub Jove aperto,* which in the month of January tendeth to the congealing of the blood in the extremities of the limbs. So out we went. T—— E—— and myself. Posted the sentries, lit a fire, and stood chatting around it till about ten, when it evanesced; so we wrapped ourselves up in our cloaks, and slept till daybreak.

Jan. 19—Two of the Sikh Sirdars came over to us to-day; one of them, Elahee Bux, commands the Sikh artillery. From their account, with a couple of hours' more daylight, we should have totally routed them. Shere Singh and a great portion of the army had gone across the river, and were brought back the next morning: they say our artillery did fearful execution, and they considered that it was all up with them. We lost all our band instruments, our canteen, and our treasure-chest—no private property, however, is missing. Sales are going on, daily, of dead officers' effects, which go for one eighth of their value—a piece of injustice both to a man's friends and to his creditors. But it can't be helped.

Jan. 20—Found a snake under my bed this morning, and took the liberty of killing him. Two of the 9th Lancers who were taken prisoners the other day, were sent back this morning with Shere Singh's compliments. They seemed rather sorry to come back, as they had been treated like princes, *pilawed* with champagne and brandy to the masthead, and sent away with ten rupees each in his pocket. Shere Singh is evidently providing for the worst, and making as favourable an impression as he can. The Sirdars are a fine set of fellows enough; it is only the rabble that perpetrate all these atrocities. There are six of their wounded now in our hospital, and treated with the greatest care.

Jan. 21—Divine service at eleven o'clock in the mess tent; after that took a walk out to the trenches. There is a breastwork thrown up along the face of the camp, interspersed with batteries here and there. Whilst we were down, a lot of the enemy came and attacked our cavalry picket, and fired at the videttes. However, a nine-pounder shot pitched into the middle of them was very persuasive, and they quickly went to the right-about. We are expecting an attack every night and day, and are all ready for them. By the bye, I have been lucky enough to procure a decent tent. B—— has bought a new one, and lent me his old one. I should surely have been laid up if I had continued in my own little *memento mori*.

Jan. 22—A very miserably juicy day, raining like a water-pot—very dark and very wretched. What an influence a wet day has on a man's mind! You remember how out of sorts I used to be at home, when I could not get out; so you can form a feeble picture of what I am now, where, instead of a large house, a warm fire, &c, I have a small comfortless tent, no carpet, damp ground, all up and down like a small common—no table, a chair without a back, and a bed with rickety legs. If I wish to go over to the mess tent, I have to wade across a place like the Slough of Despond, stumbling over tent-ropes, slipping into holes, scratching myself in bushes, and arriving there wet through, and finding everything just as miserable as what I left. The camp is a regular lake. I was obliged to make a spindle-shanked Hindu carry me over to breakfast—and what did the ill-favoured heathen do, but drop me into the midst of the deepest pool. So, of course, I rolled him in the mud to make all quits, and arrived at mess about twice as wet and dirty as I should have been if I had walked. Dined with T—— in his tent, and had a comfortable chat. About nine I attempted to get home—it was as dark as a wolfs mouth; and after half-an-hour's stumbling about up to my knees, through mud and water, I found myself, I don't know where. The rain was pouring down all the time, the wind was blowing me almost backwards, and I couldn't see a yard before me. I never was in such a fix in my life; it took me a good hour to find my tent, and when I did, I was quite done up. Obliged to sleep in my clothes, according to order—so lay down, and pulling off my boots, dropped off. The rain continued all night without intermission. I never witnessed anything like it, even in the rains. If there had been an attack, I don't believe a man in the camp would have heard it.

Jan. 23—Raining all day.

Jan. 24—Fine weather at last. Obliged, however, to keep quiet, as I have strained a set of muscles by over-exertion. My legs are not my own this morning, and I hobble about most ludicrously. I begin also to suffer from rheumatism, and must try and look out for a cheap blanket, or I shall be unfit for service. Towards evening, the Sikhs fired a salute of twenty-one guns: I suppose some other blackguard has joined them. With the battery spy-glass one can see beautifully into their camp, and nice work they are evidently preparing for us. Large parties are working perpetually, throwing up defences. A fresh battery appears every day. The Chief held a council of war today.

Jan. 25—Not very well. About two o'clock there was an alarm, and my company was ordered out on advanced picket. Took out my miserable old tent, and arranged ourselves for the night. At sunset we were visited by the brigadier, and received orders, in case of an attack, to hold our position until most of us were killed, and then to retire on the breastwork in rear. Dined in the dark, as a candle in my tent is a luxury I have not enjoyed this whole march, and then lay down in my clothes. At ten o'clock, it began to pour with rain, and lasted without a lull all night. At two I had to go my rounds, and of course got wet through; came back, and lay down again—though, for all the protection my canvass was, I might as well have been in the open air. The tent rocked to and fro, at every gust

75

of wind; the water rushed through its many apertures, and I expected it down every moment: however, that didn't hinder me from falling fast asleep, and sleeping soundly till morning.

Jan. 26—Woke at daybreak. Still raining violently. The tent was so flooded that the water rose half-way up the legs of my bed, on the top of which I lay very much in the position of the ark on Mount Ararat. Not being able to rise, I made the best of my position, and went to sleep again. At eight o'clock it ceased, and the sun came out brightly. The clouds all cleared away rapidly, and slunk off, as if they were ashamed of having spent a night in persecuting three harmless subalterns and a company of unfortunate Europeans. Waded out of my tent, and fished about till I found a piece of ground, on which I stood to get dry—breakfasted there, and then lay down on my bed, and read till the sun had dried up the greater portion of the surrounding pools. At two o'clock a royal salute, thundered out from our big guns, announced the welcome intelligence of the fall of Mooltan. I was looking through the glass at the Sikh camp, and I could see, as the loud report from the heavies came booming through the air, it seemed to swarm with human beings. Thousands on thousands seemed to be rushing about, evidently not knowing what to make of it. Bowie, one of our politicals, came into our camp today on parole, with a proposition from Shere Singh as to terms; but the only terms we can give them, I suspect, they will find hard to swallow, without a little more fighting—namely, unconditional surrender and giving up all their guns. He says that Shere Singh treats him like a brick: he has twenty men to guard him all day and night—and, such is their idea of us, a bottle of brandy is placed on his breakfast-table every morning. They boast that they are not at all afraid of us, and, if it were not for those madmen of Europeans, they would thrash our sepoys hollow.

Jan. 27—Breakfasted in bed, and kept quiet till evening. Dined at Major T——'s. Met Captain B—— there, and had a long chat with him about Warwickshire. Mounted a horse, and picked my way back through the mud to our camp about a mile off. The Sikhs fired a regular salute in honour of the new moon this evening, and kept it up the greater part of the night.

CHAPTER 5

Camp at Russool

Feb. 3, Camp, Chilianwalla—Since I sent off my last packet, I have been spending my time very pleasantly in bed, amusing myself with lotions, leeches, and the doctor. I am now allowed to sit up for a short time, because I have nothing to lie down on—seeing that my bed, having long been screwed on its pins, last night, as, in my dreams, I was fighting a single combat with a dozen or more Sikhs, just as I made a furious lunge, and skivered a fellow, of a sudden gave way with a crash, and awoke me most disagreeably to the realities of life by depositing my back on the corner of a box. Therefore, whilst my couch is being repaired, I will give you a short account of what has been going on in these last few days. The treasure taken at Mooltan, amounts, it is said, to some three millions of pounds—rather a considerable sum, and all lawful prize-money. General Whish is on his way up, by the other bank of the Jhelum, and will join us soon. The Sikhs are very noisy, and very busy: they have shifted their position considerably. We also have been hard at work throwing up batteries, redoubts, &c, as it is supposed that Shere Singh may screw up his courage to attack us before General Whish arrives. Brigadier Godby is removed to take command at Lahore, and we are to have somebody else, which we are all very sorry for. One of our cavalry pickets had a small skirmish with the enemy yesterday, and drove them back.

Feb. 5—Still in bed, and how sick I am of it I need not say. I don't think I have ever been confined so long before, except when I broke my leg; and if it was wearying work at home, you may imagine what it is here, poring over one well-read book—rejected at any other time for its extreme dullness, but now read over and over again in vain search for amusement—counting the patterns of the tent, enumerating the holes in the roof, the irregularities in the floor, the pieces of paper strewn about; speculating on the doctor's next visit, looking longingly at the bright sunshine outside, and the cricket-bat in the corner of the tent; playing half a tune on the flute, and laying it down in disgust; and then, when the shades of evening come down, and everything is dull and gloomy, lying awake and listening to the howling of the jackals, who congregate in troops on the battle-field in front, or to the challenge of the sentry; and counting the lazy hours as they creep along. Oh! it is a lively thing—a sickbed in camp! Nothing particular has occurred today, except the detection of a Baboo in the Chief's office, who is said to have been in the habit of sending over to Shere Singh a copy of every order that has been issued since the commencement of the campaign—so that not a movement have we made that the enemy has not been acquainted with beforehand: that accounts for the excellence of their manoeuvres. The rascal has escaped to their camp. At the redoubt, there is amusement going on in the sharp-shooting line—the Sikhs creeping out, and firing at our sentries, and the pickets returning the compliment. The duty is very heavy; more than half the regiment is under arms every day. I wish that General Whish and his force would arrive—only let me get on my pins first.

Feb. 6—Couldn't stand the confinement any longer, so have persuaded the doctor to let me crawl about a little. Colonel Godby has gone to Lahore, and Brigadier

Penny has command of our brigade. It is getting near the hot weather, and many are the conjectures as to our future movements. ... If the next fight is a decisive one, we shall perhaps return to cantonments; but still a large force will have to be kept on the frontier. Perhaps we shall stay where we are, and make a bit of a station. Pretty living that will be! I think I can see the house of my constructing, in which I shall have to swelter through the hot weather. I expect that either here or at Lahore will be the summer quarters of what are left of us: however, "sufficient for the day is the evil thereof." That's true: indeed, it generally *is*. The pickets are popping away very lively in front—another scrimmage, I suppose. These Sikh gentry never give us any peace. They have moved their camp considerably more over to our right, and have evidently got some cunning dodge on the *tapis*. I wish they would do something. I never so thoroughly felt before the misery of idleness—*forced* idleness as it is: I suppose that's what makes it so disagreeable. I have no occupation for mind or body, except thought; and what is there to think of? I think of home—it gives me the blues; I think of India—it gives me the spleen; of my future prospects—not cheering; the next fight—chance of being knocked over—not comforting. If I escape—a hot season, *sub Jove aperto*—probably get liver, or cholera, or dysentery—all enlivening! It's no good thinking. So I try to do something—take up *Chambers's Journal,* open a place I know by heart, throw it down, and take up a pen; try to write, but feel too stupid to write to you, and too much out of sorts for anything else; throw that down, and get my flute; begin to play mechanically some old air that reminds me of home, and leave off with a sigh; crawl out of my tent, and into somebody else's: find the worthy occupant just as *ennuyé* as myself—lying on his bed and spitting on the floor, by way of amusement. Sit down opposite him, and look at him for a few minutes—then give a yawn and go out. Wander somewhere else, and find the next man smoking like a steam-engine, and looking at the ceiling—ask him how he is, and he returns the compliment. After that, conversation flags—stay about two minutes, and then bolt—and so on through the camp. I feel myself getting duller and duller, stupider and stupider, every day. A lively addition I shall make to the family circle when I come home! So, if you ever meet a very stupid Indian officer, and you, my fair sisters, are inclined to turn up your noses at him, substitute pity for contempt: he was probably a very sharp boy when he left home—considered, perhaps, the genius of the family—until for want of nourishment the flame went out, and he became, in the general stagnation, as torpid as the rest. Mooned about all day. Went to mess, brightened up a little, discussed military topics with ——.

Feb. 7—Much better. Wrote to the doctor to put me off the sick-list. Rode out to the advanced picket, visited the officer on duty. Had a few balls at cricket, like a fool as I was, and returned to camp. Spent a pleasant evening. Men brighten up at dinner-time.

Feb. 8—Up early. Went out to join my company at the redoubt—a strong fortified work thrown up to our right about a quarter of a mile—where we have our light field-battery, two companies of our regiment, and two of the 70th. The enemy have divided their force, and have a large body of men in our rear, and likewise on our right. Their object evidently is to entice us to attack them, and decide the question before Whish comes up; but it won't do. The Sikhs have a large picket in sight, on the top of a low range of hills, and their impudence is increasing daily. There is a small village, about five hundred yards in front of the redoubt, which we hold for the sake of a well there;

and they come down in swarms, creeping through the jungle until they are about a hundred yards off, and then blaze away at us with their matchlocks—which is anything but agreeable, as you cannot show yourself without having a dozen balls whistling over your head. They have just walked off with a flock of goats right under our noses—the camp-followers will, in spite of injunctions, drive their cattle out beyond the pickets, and the consequence is, that they are continually being carried off. At sunset, dressed—ready to receive the Chief, who pays a visit here every evening with General Gilbert, when he takes a long look at the enemy, asks a multitude of questions difficult to be answered, communeth with his staff, and departs. There are six of us down here—Major Talbot in command—and we make a very pleasant party. Were smoking our cheroots after dinner, when we were told that, instead of sleeping comfortably in our beds, as we supposed, E—— ——, T——, and myself were to go down and relieve one another in charge of the village. So, at nine o'clock, off we marched all together—our niggers, with our beds, bringing up the rear—posted the sentries round the village; and, as E—— had first watch, T—— and I lay down, and went to sleep. Had not lain half-an-hour when it began to rain—so we had to bundle our beds into a small *faqueer's* hut, where we had the company of about twenty sepoys; so that, altogether, we were pretty closely packed. However, I managed to sleep sound. At eleven, T—— relieved E——, who went back to camp; at two, I relieved T——. It had cleared up, and was a beautiful moonlight night. Visited the sentries, and walked about the village in conversation with the Surbadar. Three of the enemy's horsemen passed close by, but, for fear of alarming the camp, I wouldn't allow the sentry to fire. I could have knocked over one with the greatest ease.

82

Feb. 9—Went down to the village. Spent the night as the last, except that we had our beds in the open air.

Feb. 10—Received your letter. Delighted beyond measure at the good news about C——. I am as proud as Punch, and as happy as a king; and only lament that I have no one here to rejoice with me; so I must even keep the joyful intelligence to myself, and vent my exultation in a few private capers in my own tent. I am more pleased than if I had been presented with a staff appointment, or made a knight in presence of the army. Nightingale is doing well. His is a miraculous recovery. He went off yesterday with the rest of the wounded to the provinces, on his way home. We expect General Whish's force about the 20th, and then we will teach these gentlemen a lesson—if they don't give in beforehand, which they don't seem inclined to do. We shall have a hundred pieces of artillery. Just fancy the noise they'll make in the land. The Sikhs have a strong position, though; and all sorts of agreeable things, in the shape of entrenchments, batteries, and mines, they have in pickle for us on that hill.

Feb. 11—Put on the sick-list again, I am sorry to say. My expedition to the redoubt has not done me any good. Ordered to keep my bed, to which, however, the fates were not propitious; for, about half-past ten, three guns, fired from the heavy battery on the mound, gave the alarm; and of course, in spite of the doctor, out I turned—threw on my clothes, sword, and pistols, and joined the regiment at the alarm-post. The whole army was under arms in less than ten minutes. The foe, they said, were coming down upon us—but after waiting out an hour, not a bit of an enemy could I see; so, being on the sick-list, I returned to my tent. Lord Gough was out in the rear today, with some cavalry and horse artillery, and had a small scrimmage with

83

the enemy, in which a few of them were knocked over. An offer of free pardon was sent over today, I hear, to all the rebels, provided they give up their guns, and come and deposit their arms in front of our camp—Shere Singh and his father to be allowed money to live on, but no territory. Of course, they won't accept these terms without another thrashing. In bed again, and about as comfortable as a tied-up pointer, or, if you like the simile better, a chained eagle. I have but this moment discovered that today is Sunday—being away on duty, and having nothing here to mark that day more than any other. If it were not for my journal, I should not know the day of the week or month. I told you, I believe, that the Sikhs carried off our band instruments the other day, so that we have nothing now but our fifes and drums. It is a loss of four thousand rupees to us; however, it can't be helped.

Feb. 12—Here I am dressed for the day—on my bed—with a borrowed table at my side, on which lie my desk, my pistols, and a bottle of lotion—a pipe and a Shakespeare. I have just taken my breakfast. Cold tea, milkless and sugarless, stands at my elbow, into which I occasionally dive for refreshment; and now, to while away the weary hours, I will go on with my journal. I was dreaming of home all last night, and awoke with the impression so vividly on my mind, that I could hardly shake it off. The Sikhs have all of a sudden abandoned their strong position at Russool, and gone off to the right. The only reason that can be supposed for their evacuating a place of such great strength is, that they were unable to procure sufficient supplies for their immense army. As soon as they were off, General Gilbert, and a lot of officers from our camp, galloped over to see it; and, from all accounts, it's a good thing for us that they have abandoned it; as, if resolutely defended, it could not have been carried without fearful loss. First, there was a long breastwork dotted with batteries, extending for a good mile. In front of this there was a deep ravine; and close on the trench an immense barrier of thorns, which must have brought up our infantry for a time; whilst a heavy fire would have been poured into them from the very muzzles of the guns;—that gained, there was ravine after ravine for a quarter of a mile, with only one or two narrow paths, and the whole raked by their guns on the heights. The sides of the ravine were all scarped down, so as to be insurmountable; and to have toiled through these obstacles, all the time exposed to their murderous fire, would have been terrific work. At last came the village of Russool, on the summit of a crag some sixty feet high, sheer perpendicular on all sides, and covered with batteries—only one narrow pass up to it, where scarce eight men could walk abreast; and this could have been destroyed by them in a short time. Of course we should have taken it if we had attacked it; but there would have been few to rejoice at the victory. I am not good at describing a strong position; but this, all the generals say, was a tremendous one. However, they're out of it now. Several men have just come in from the battlefield; the bodies of the dead are still lying there in heaps, and poisoning the air; the jackals howl all night over their loathsome banquet. Such are the horrors perpetrated by man for a few miles of land, a quibble in a treaty, or a short-lived glory. God! how is glory obtained, that men should be so proud of it!

Thus ends my journal for this stupid fortnight; however, you cannot expect a general action every packet. There will probably be one in the next.

P.S. Feb. 14—I hear this morning that Shere Singh has been fool enough to run his head into the snare, by going back to Wuzeerabad. I hope it's true—an open country and no favour!

CHAPTER 6

Battle of Gujarat

Feb. 13, Camp, Chilianwalla—Still confined to this weary bed, by these tedious swellings. I shall let them take their own course in a few days, if they don't get better. The Sikhs have all moved away, and gone, no one knows where. However, we shall hear in a few hours, as we have reconnoitring parties out.

Feb. 14—Just finished, and sent off my despatch, when an order came down for us to march in an hour, as the Sikhs had gone round our rear, and are, they say, marching on Lahore. Got up and dressed, and went over to the mess to get some food before starting. All the tents were struck—and we waited about two hours in the sun, expecting to march—when the movement of the troops was countermanded till tomorrow morning. Pitched my tent, and got into bed again; not at all benefited, as you may suppose, by the exercise. If Shere Singh has really marched on Lahore, he is playing a very bold game, and we must look sharp, or he'll get there before us. It may be only a ruse of theirs; however, we shall see. Stayed in bed all day rather impatiently. There will be some work to be done soon, and I am by no means in working condition; however, if I am carried, I will go with the corps.

Feb. 15—At four o'clock the advance sounded, and off we marched from the ground on which we expected to have decided the campaign. Until the sun rose it was very cold—and the road was strewed with dead bodies of camels, horses, and oxen, making the atmosphere almost pestilential. At eight it grew hot, and towards midday awfully so. After having been confined so long, I could not stand the heat—my head felt like lead—and I thought I should have dropped from my horse two or three times. I saw one horse-artilleryman fall heavily to the ground, and lie there senseless, struck by a *coup-de-soleil*. At one o'clock we got clear of the dreadful jungle: I hope I may never see its face again. At half-past two, we arrived at Lussoura, after a march of twenty miles, the most fatiguing we have had yet; and there we halted. Stuck my sword in the ground, and put my cloak on the top of it, to make a sort of covering for my head, till the arrival of my traps—then tied a wet towel round my head, and lay down with a racking headache, and my swellings much inflamed: however, a couple of hours' sleep set me all right.

Feb. 16—Marched at five. The doctor gave me a *doolie*, so I was carried along very comfortably. The march was only seven miles, and we got to our ground, Sadoolapoor—where the action was fought on the 3rd of December—before it got hot. Whish was to have joined us today; and we are to march on again in the night twenty miles to Gujerat, where the enemy are said to be.

Evening—We do not march tonight, as Whish has not joined us.

Feb. 17—We had been ordered to halt today; but about eight o'clock an order came for us to strike our tents, and after swallowing a hasty breakfast we marched. Went along in a *doolie*, all ready to turn out, in case of there being anything to be done. However, the march passed off quietly—we only went seven miles, and then pitched our camp. The 10th Queen's and 52nd N.I., from Mooltan, joined us this morning; the rest of General Whish's force are behind, but expected tomorrow, or the next day. We shall probably not wait for them. We all anticipate fighting next morning.

Feb. 18—Marched about nine; and after a tramp of about eight miles, pitched our camp within three miles of the enemy. We expect to go at them fresh tomorrow morning; but there's no saying. The 8th N.I. arrived in the night.

Afternoon—There is a sudden rumour that Shere Singh has fled with 4000 men.

Evening—Still rumoured that Shere Singh has given us leg-bail; but I don't believe it myself. Elephants have been sent to bring up the 53rd Queen's, 60th Rifles, and the 1st Bombay Fusileers. We wait here for them tomorrow—and then I opine we shall go and knock this place Gujarat down about the Sikhs' ears. Nothing occurred today, except hanging two or three camp-followers for plundering.

Feb. 19—Halted all day. This is a beautifully rich and fertile country: for miles and miles round there is nothing but luxuriant green corn-fields. I am pitched right in the centre of one, and have a soft verdant carpet under my feet. Just imagine the damage an army like this must do to the crops. The 60th Rifles, 1st Bombay Fusileers, and 32nd foot have arrived; Markham's brigade, and the rest of Whish's force will come in the evening; and then we shall have altogether about 25,000 men, and more than a hundred pieces of artillery.

Feb. 20—Here I am again: we have not fought yet, but there is little doubt but that we shall engage tomorrow—and then won't there be a smash! We marched at one o'clock today, and have moved up close, so as to go at them fresh in the morning, and have lots of time to complete the victory. The artillery, twenty-two heavy guns, are to open at 1200 yards—then the whole line at 800, 600, 400, 200—and then let loose the infantry. The cavalry have been ordered not to draw rein until their horses drop in the pursuit. Tippoo is counting his chickens before they're hatched, you will say; however, the event will show. And now, goodbye. God bless you all! "A soldier's grave, or a thousand merks," as Mr Bothwell says in *Old Mortality*.

Feb. 22.—Here I am again, hungry, thirsty, and tired; but, thank God, all right. I have not tasted food for eight-and-forty hours, barring a brace of hard-boiled eggs, which I got hold of at half-past twelve o'clock today—and therefore I am rather faint; but we have cooked Shere Singh's goose, and now I will tell you all about it.

Feb. 21—At half-past five turned out of bed—dressed; and then, regardless of expense, considering the occasion, brewed a large *jorum* of tea with sugar and milk—unwonted luxuries, but very consoling in the raw morning. Spent an hour strolling about and chatting with those around. Everyone seems to be in remarkably good spirits, and more amiable than wont, when there is a chance of your place being empty before night. Those whom at other times you hardly exchange a word with, come in now for a cordial good-morning; and towards your friends the moment seems to draw you closer, and make your heart expand with greater warmth.

Well, at seven o'clock we were all under arms, and the Chief cantered down the whole line, receiving the cheers of each regiment as he passed. At half-past seven we advanced in order of battle, quarter-distance; column of brigade at wheeling distance; the heavy guns in the centre, and the light field batteries at intervals along the line, with the horse-artillery and cavalry on either flank.

I went along in my *doolie* for the first three miles; indeed, I was in great pain, and I wanted to save my strength until required. At last a gun fired from the enemy's outpost told me it was time to be stirring; and, luckily for me, as I jumped from my *doolie*, both my wounds burst at once, and I was relieved immediately, and able to walk without pain. I mounted a horse, and rode along with my regiment, until the order came to load, fix bayonets, and wheel into line— when we all dismounted, and joined our companies. . . .

(But I am so sick for want of food, that I must leave off till I have devoured some of the half-cooked viands I expect directly. . . . I have eaten, and am filled, and the tea-kettle is hissing merrily, so I hope soon to get something to drink: the water here is so thick with mud that a horse would refuse it.)

After we had wheeled into line, we advanced about a quarter of a mile, and then the enemy opened on us from the whole of the front. The round-shot flew about us, and ploughed up the ground in all directions. Five or six men were knocked down in as many seconds, when we were ordered to lie down, and the artillery advanced about two hundred yards to the front—the big guns opening first— and instantly the roar of more than a hundred pieces of artillery shook the very earth, pitching round-shot and shells into the enemy from less than three hundred yards, they returning our fire with great spirit and precision.

At the end of an hour, we were ordered to advance another hundred yards, and then lie down again. A company from each regiment in the brigade was sent up to the front to support the troop of horse-artillery attached to us; and, poor fellows, they suffered dreadfully, being brought in, one after another, wounded—some with legs shot off, some cut in half, some torn with grape—until scarcely half of our rifle company was left.

All this time the fire was very hot on us, carrying off three men at a time, shells bursting over us, or burying themselves in front, scattering the earth in our faces. There was a constant line of *doolies* from our regiment to the hospital, as, one after another, the men were carried off. The troop in front (Fordyce's) suffered dreadfully—every shot pitched right into them; and the gallant manner in which they worked their guns is beyond all praise. Twice had they to retire to the rear for fresh horses and men, and each time as they came up again, and passed through our line, we gave them a hearty cheer; and the fine fellows waved their caps, and dashed on again in advance, as if death was a joke to them.

This lasted about two hours—during which time the enemy's fire was evidently slackening—when a very annoying fire was opened upon us from a village about two hundred yards in front, and our brigade was ordered on to storm it. Our men, who had been held down all this time, started up with a cheer. It was the last some of them gave, poor fellows! A round-shot took off a man's head close to me, and spattered his brains in my face—the bullets whizzing about like hail—and as we came nearer, grape was poured into us, but not a man wavered for a second.

"Officers to the front—Lead on your men!" shouted the major; and we sprang forward amidst a shower of balls, dashed across a deep *nullah*, gave one rattling volley, and poured into the village at every point. Many of the Sikhs stood and fought like men, but the greater portion (there must have been at least 1000) left the village at one end as we entered at the other. Those who remained were shot or bayoneted on the spot. There was no quarter given. A number of them shut themselves up in the houses, but our men beat down the doors, and poured in volley after volley, and sullenly and savagely they died fighting to the last. We captured three of their standards in the village—and then, leaving the left wing to keep possession, we defiled to the right; and found ourselves under a hot fire of grape and canister, totally unsupported, as we had advanced in front of the whole line to storm the village, and the troop of horse-artillery had been obliged to retire, being temporarily disabled.

This was the most deadly fire we were exposed to during the day, the balls hissing about like winged serpents. I was talking to Sprot, and made some remark about the fire, and he answered me with a smile, and I turned my head to watch Fordyce's troop of horse-artillery coming up again to our support; when I looked round, Sprot was lying at my feet in his blood. I tried to raise him, but he was stone-dead. A ball had struck him on the back of the head, and had entered the brain. And there he lay—the finest young fellow in the corps—the life and soul of the mess, beloved by all—struck down in his prime. The smile was still on his lips as when he spoke to me last; and but for the blood that bedabbled his curling hair, and the cold blue hue about his lips and eyelids, you would have fancied him in a peaceful sleep—so calm, so painless was the expression of his countenance. He was one of my chief friends; but it was no time for lamentation; and after taking one long gaze at his pallid face, a moment ago so full of life and manly beauty, I rejoined my company.

A troop of horse-artillery dashed past us at a gallop, drew up, unlimbered, and returned the enemy's fire. The whole line of infantry was seen advancing; our guns poured in a withering fire; the enemy left theirs and fled. The cavalry charged in amongst them, and the horse-artillery rattled on at a gallop, mowing them down in heaps, while we took possession of their guns and camp, leaving the cavalry to deal with the fugitives; and awful execution they did amongst them, as we afterwards heard. The 3rd and 14th Dragoons, 9th Lancers, Scinde horse, and all the regular and irregular cavalry, pursued them with the horse-artillery for ten miles, and cut them down by hundreds. Not a rein was drawn till the horses could go no further; their sabres drank deep of blood that day, and they returned wearied and jaded, and glutted with slaughter. No attempt was made at rallying—the rout was complete—and long will the Sikhs have cause to remember the battle of Gujarat.

The whole line of their flight was strewed with dead. We advanced into their camp over heaps of dead and dying. It wanted nothing more to show the gallant stand they had made. Everything was in confusion—tumbrels overturned, guns dismounted, wagons with their wheels off, oxen and camels rushing wildly about, wounded horses plunging in their agony, beds, blankets, boxes, ammunition, strewed about the ground in a perfect chaos; the wounded lying there groaning, some begging to be despatched, others praying for mercy, and some, with scowling looks of impotent rage, striving to cut down those who came near them, and thereby insuring their own destruction—for but little quarter, I am ashamed to say, was given—and even those we managed to save from the vengeance of our men were, I fear, killed afterwards. But, after all, it is a war of extermination.

The most heartrending sight of the day was one I witnessed in a tent I entered. There, on the ground, bleeding to death, lay a young mother; her leg had been carried off by a round-shot, and the jagged stump protruded in a ghastly manner through the mangled flesh. She held a baby to her breast—and as she bent over it with maternal anxiety, all her thoughts seemed to be of her child. She appeared totally regardless of the agony she must have been suffering, and to think of nothing but the poor infant which was drawing its nourishment from her failing breast. I gave her some water—and she drank it greedily, raising her large imploring eyes to my face with an expression that was heart-rending to witness. I was obliged to leave the poor creature, and go on with the regiment; but the remembrance of that sight will live with me till my dying day.

After we had spiked all the guns, and sent them to the rear, we advanced about a mile, and there halted, and commenced collecting the enemy's ammunition, which was scattered about in immense quantities all over the field. They had been unable to carry anything off, so rapid had been our advance, and there was powder and shot lying everywhere in heaps, enough to replenish all the magazines in Europe.

About this time a horrid accident took place. Two of our men, and four sepoys of the 70th, in the unthinking way peculiar to the lower classes, went and sat down by one of the ammunition wagons we had captured—when the Europeans took out their pipes, and began to smoke; a spark communicated with the powder, and the whole blew up, leaving these six poor fellows hopelessly scorched on the ground. One man's head was blown off, and he was the happiest of the whole—for the agony the others must have suffered is indescribable. One of them started up and commenced running about all in flames, until, overcome with the torment, he fell to the ground. All this time no one dared go near him, as his ammunition-pad was in a blaze, and had not yet exploded. It was fearful to see the flames eating into his vitals, and his unavailing struggles to free himself from them. At last, I saw a piece of a tent lying on the ground, which I snatched up and threw over him; but there was no hope for him. All of them, in their agony, had torn off every stitch of clothing; and the black and scorched flesh hanging in strips—their withered tongues protruding from their mouths, in which the blood was gurgling, as they gasped for breath—their faces like blackened masks, and their eyes starting from their sockets—their groans, and the screams for water, with which they pointed to their parched mouths, showed a frightful picture of some of the horrors attendant upon war. They were all taken to the hospital instantly; but none was likely to recover. I hope I may never witness such a sight again—excruciating suffering without the power of rendering assistance.

The Commander-in-chief came down the line just after this catastrophe, and we stood to our arms and cheered him as he passed. He expressed himself highly pleased with our regiment, and told Major Steele he might be proud of us. After he had passed, the major gave us a short speech, and told us to salute the colours, as we had done them honour. We then piled arms, and I went over to the hospital.

We have suffered fearfully—nearly one hundred and fifty killed and wounded, out of little more than four hundred. After speaking cheerily to the wounded men, poor fellows! as they lay on the ground with their mangled limbs, (they seemed grateful for any kindness, and brightened up so when any of their officers came near them, that it made one's heart swell,) I passed on from *doolie* to *doolie*, looking at all the patients. Some, alas! whose stiffened forms showed their state, were past speaking too; others were in too great pain to be sensible; but many, I am glad to say, seemed likely to do well; and several men, whose legs had been taken off, lay smoking their pipes and chatting to their comrades, as unconcernedly as if nothing had happened.

At last I came to poor Sprot's *doolie*; he lay there just as he fell—so calm and natural, he looked as if you could wake him with a touch—save that the ashy hue of death had already begun to spread over his face. How full of life he was in the morning, and look upon him now! I sat by him for some time, till they came to lay him out; and then I cut a button from his jacket as a keepsake, and left him. After this I went to the doctor to have my hand dressed, for I am amongst the slightly wounded, having been hit with a grape-shot in the left hand, and having a piece taken out of my right wrist; however, you see I can write, so it isn't very bad.

At sunset our camp arrived, and I pitched my tent; but there was no food to be got—so I dined off a cup of tea. At night, there was one of the most beautiful sights I ever saw. All the enemy's ammunition that had been taken, was blown up in different parts of the field: every moment a thundering explosion shook the ground, and lit up the whole heavens. There must have been nearly a thousand of them, for they lasted all night. I did not get to sleep for a long time, for I was over-tired from the violent exercise and excitement, after being confined so long, and my thigh pained me very much; but about three o'clock, I managed to drop over. And this ends the battle of Gujarat, one of the most decisive fought in India. We have taken sixty of the enemy's guns—which were all they had with them—and totally routed them, with comparatively little loss; although we don't yet know the amount.

Feb. 22—We had expected to halt after the hard work of yesterday, and, indeed, the troops needed it; but at nine o'clock, before we could get any food, our division, commanded by General Gilbert, and the Bombay forces, were ordered to march in pursuit, and take possession of the Pooran pass—that place in the hills I mentioned in my last. After swallowing a cup of tea, off we started, leaving our wounded behind, and marched all day through a blazing sun. The men suffered fearfully for want of water. After marching about fifteen miles, many of them dropped down; the road was strewed with Europeans and sepoys; and not a drop of water could be obtained. Our men stood it the best, but they were greatly distressed; and when we arrived, after twenty-five miles, at our halting place for the night, everyone was knocked up. It may seem strange to you that men should be so fatigued with marching twenty-five miles, but they had hardly tasted food since yesterday morning—they had no water, and were under an Indian sun. A little after sunset our tents came up, when I got the first meal I had tasted for forty-eight hours. I could not get any water to wash with, though—it was too precious, dirty as it was; however, I managed to get a cup of tea, after which I sat up writing to you until it struck twelve.

Feb. 23—In the middle of last night, or rather about two o'clock this morning, the storm, which a heavy cannonading almost always brings on, came down; and I was awakened from a sound sleep by the tent being blown down about my ears, and being nearly suffocated in the folds. Anything like the fury of the storm, I never could have imagined; it was a regular hurricane. The wind roared in a most frightful manner; the loose ropes flogged the canvass with a noise like thunder; the rain came down in torrents, and all was confusion and uproar through all the camp—everyone's tent either down, or else in great danger. The shouting of the niggers, the swearing of the Europeans, the kicking of the horses, the flapping of canvass, and the roaring of the tempest, made as pretty a Babel of utter confusion as you would wish to hear. De M—— and myself cowered down under the wet folds of the tent, and waited patiently till it should give over. I was so tired out that I don't believe I should have cared for anything; and I actually fell asleep in the midst of it, and did not awake until morning, when the storm had lulled: but there was still a miserable cold, cutting wind, and we started on the march anything but comfortable. Marched along all day, the men keeping up bravely. Nothing seems to tire them. Last night they didn't appear able to go another mile; and today they came along as fresh as ever. At one o'clock we reached the pass. The Bombay division halted at the entrance, and we went on through it—and a most formidable gorge it appeared to be: a thousand men could have held it against an army, there being only one narrow path through it, and that very rough and broken. How we got our guns through, I can't imagine. The scenery was superb—wild, and picturesque,—but we were not able to enjoy it; for, just in the centre of the pass, a tremendous storm of wind and rain, mingled with hail, came on, and we were wet to the skin. The thunder was awful, and seemed just above our heads. The pass was three miles long, and heartily glad we were when we reached the extremity, and got into the open country. We marched about another mile, making sixteen in all, and then halted—rain still pouring down, and a cold wind cutting us nearly in two: it was very miserable, I can assure you. We had then to wait a good two hours before our tents arrived, not having tasted food all day—so that there was a regular rush towards the mess camels when they made their appearance. I cut off a piece of half-raw beef as big as my fist, and devoured it on the spot, so hungry was I.

Feb. 24—At nine o'clock marched for the town of Jhelum on the river, where we received information that a party of the Sikhs were trying to cross with some three or four guns. Passed a number of them lying dead in the road, evidently cut up by the cavalry in advance. Arrived at our ground, close to the banks of the river, about five o'clock. The enemy have been too quick for us, and are over with their guns on the other side, commanding the ford with them, so that we cannot cross with our small force. They have ten thousand men, and about thirty guns, which they had left there formerly; so I suppose we shall wait here for the Bombay division to come up. Indeed, I doubt if we can go on—the gun horses are all completely knocked up, and so are the men. Our baggage arrived soon after us, and I spent a more comfortable evening, and got a better dinner than I have had for some time. After all, there is a good deal of pleasure in this style of life; because, when you do get comfortable, it is such clover.

Feb. 25—A halt. I saw Major Tait yesterday; he says the cavalry must have cut down thousands. Poor wretches! they have got little reward for their service. Shere Singh was to have paid them after they had thrashed us; they have none of them received anything yet, nor are likely. The enemy are very busy burning their boats on the other side of the river. Some of our artillery were ordered down to pepper them, but not a troop or battery was able to move: all the horses are completely done up. We don't know what is to be done next; but I can't think there will be any more fighting to signify. It will soon be awfully hot. We have not yet ascertained our exact loss; but it must be considerable—twenty-five killed and wounded in my own company alone, out of forty men. The whole loss of the army is estimated at about five hundred, out of which three hundred were in our brigade, which was almost the only one actively engaged.

Feb. 26—Halting still. We have lots of work before us. I hear that scoundrel, Dost Mohammed, has joined the Sikhs, and has brought more guns. There were numbers of the Afghans fighting against us at Gujarat—so I suppose we shall finish the campaign in Peshawar. A son of Dost Mohammed was killed in the action the other day. A number of dead and wounded Sikhs have been found in the villages about here, and brought into the hospitals—poor fellows! The villagers hate them, the Sikhs having been very oppressive; and now is their time of retaliation. The Sikhs, you know, are mostly soldiers and of the Hindu persuasion, and the villagers, Mohammedans and serfs to the former, who make them do all the cultivation of the country, and levy by force and plunder the means of an idle subsistence. Our orders have come out now, and everything is settled. We are to cross the Jhelum under General Gilbert; and you will probably hear of me at Attock in a short time: so our hardships are not over yet. However, I like adventure, and rather prefer this gipsy mode of life to the routine of cantonments; besides, I hear it is a beautiful country, and grapes and apples are as cheap as dirt there—so, *en avant!* The Commander-in-chief may send us to the antipodes, if he likes, for what I care. Mark Tapley's maxims for ever!

Feb. 27—Marched at daybreak along the banks of the Jhelum about nine miles, and arrived at another ford, opposite to which we encamped. I suppose we cross tomorrow morning—the left wing of our regiment are ordered to the island tonight, to take possession of a village there. It is now evening, and I am drinking tea alone in my tent. One feeble candle stuck in a bottle renders darker surrounding objects. The green corn—for I am pitched as usual in the middle of a corn-field—rises half-way up the legs of my table; and there is a stray goat belonging to someone, very coolly regaling himself on the same. So much for the romance, of my present position. I really think I should consider myself a hero by this time, if there were not so many in the same condition. Two general actions, and the possibility of more, when six months ago we did not expect to see a shot fired. How little we can tell what's going to happen! However, I am very glad we have seen service, just to give one reason to be proud of our little corps, for other qualities than its appearance on parade; and proud I am to belong to it. A finer set of fellows never wore cross-belt; their behaviour the other day was superb, and the only difficulty was in holding them in. They seemed to look on fighting as a pastime, and were quite merry all the time. Shere Singh, I hear, is feeling very small now, and wants to come to terms. Hang him! However, he is a fine fellow in his way; although it is said he didn't trust his precious body under fire on the 21st. But now it is getting late, and we have to be up early, and cross the river—another word for wet feet, and no breakfast, I imagine. I hope my accounts won't tempt any of my brothers to make red scarecrows of themselves; *beatus ille, qui procul negotiis,* happy is he who is well out of it—though I like it amazingly myself. Good night! Barring a howling dog, a troop of jackals, and a sleepless camel outside who roars all night, all is hushed in repose.

Feb. 28—Tents struck at five, marched down to the river at six, and commenced crossing. It was a very broad swift stream, and fording was attended with considerable danger. I saw several camels swept off their legs and carried down with their loads. A lot of bullocks, also, and horses were drowned, and a few camp-followers; but our men all got safely across in about two hours. I, being on the sick-list, got over on an elephant without wetting my feet. Halted on the island for an hour or so, and then marched down to the other ford. The first was bad enough—but this was a tremendous one, about two hundred yards in breadth, very deep, and the stream running like a sluice. It was fordable only to elephants and camels without their loads. Lots of the latter, who missed the ford, were carried down the stream and drowned. Poor brutes! how they struggled. It took us the whole day to cross this place; all the camels had to be unladen, and their loads carried over on elephants; the men went over in the same way, and very slow work it was. I don't believe we ever should have effected it before night, but that about two o'clock five boats sent down by Gholab Singh arrived, and then we got on faster. As it was, it was sunset, and every man in the regiment had crossed over, before I was able to get my traps across. After I had seen the whole safe in boats, I got into one myself, and took my turn. There was no one at the other side when I reached it—they had all gone on to the camp; and not liking the idea of walking in my bad state, I looked about for the means of equestrian conveyance, and at last espied a vicious little pony, belonging to one of ours, without saddle or bridle. However, "a friend in need;" so, avoiding a dexterous attempt to bite, and another to kick me, I vaulted on his back, and set forth. Had to ford another branch of the river—shallow, but so strong that it nearly carried my little *tat* off his legs. Precious glad when I got into camp—but had to wait a good hour for my tent, the camel that carried it having lost his legs in the last ford, and fallen—so everything was wet through. "That's what I call pleasant, said Mr Brown." Took tea and turned into bed. The Sikhs have all gone from this part of the country. General Steinbach joined us today, with a lot of Gholab Singh's riff-raff.

March 1—The beginning of the hot weather, when all peaceable people are snug in cantonments: however, it is very pleasant as yet. Marched at eight, and crossed three more fords. I never saw such a river as this is: happily we are at the other side of it now; for, of all the twisting, winding, interminable streams that ever baffled patience, this is the worst. We have had to cross it six times in the space of two miles. Encamped at about a quarter of a mile distant; got something to eat. We consider ourselves lucky when we do that now; and, like Captain Dalgetty, victual ourselves for an indefinite period, when provender is within our reach. Got to bed as soon as my tent arrived, which was not until about two hours after we had reached our ground. Reason why—the camel had fallen down again in the last ford, and took a long time to get on his legs. The cattle are all getting worn out; and I expect some day to have my traps left in the jungle: however, I'm a philosopher. We march tomorrow towards Attock; the whole army is over the river by this time. The despatches are not published yet, and we have heard nothing about our future movements; there is little doubt, however, but that we are bound for Peshawar. Lay still all day. I hope soon, by keeping quiet, to be all right again; but you cannot imagine how irksome lying in bed is to me at such a stirring time. At sunset we had a tremendous storm of thunder and rain, but it did not last long. Dined with De M——, who always stays from mess, and keeps me company. Three more of our men have died of their wounds.

March 2—It rained so heavily in the night, that we are unable to march until one o'clock. Our brigade then starts alone with Dawes' battery, to take possession of Rhotas, which the Sikhs have just evacuated.

Evening—Just dined. We have had a long march; but the beautiful scenery we passed through amply repaid us. Started at one o'clock, and, after five hours' march, entered the hills that form the pass leading to Rhotas. The scenery was grandly wild and picturesque—the road the bed of a torrent, on each side of which the hills rose almost abruptly, clothed in the richest verdure—while all beneath was one tumbled mass of black rocks. The strength of the place defies description. Luckily for us, there was no enemy near, or they might have peppered us nicely. After about three miles, the pass grew so narrow that not more than four could walk abreast. The ascent became very steep also; and on turning a corner we came in sight of the fort of Rhotas—a magnificent structure, reminding one of the castles of old, situated at the summit of a towering hill, and commanding a view of the whole of the surrounding country. To it we advanced by a narrow defile, hewn out of the solid rock, and overtopped by beetling crags, from which we should have been exposed to a raking fire if there had been an enemy, which happily there was not. The path wound along under the walls of the fort for half a mile, and then we gained the summit, and the principal gate of the place. Some of us went in to see the interior, but the brigade passed on, and descended by the same narrow defile to the plain on the other side. Walked all over the fort; it is a place of immense natural strength, and at the time in which it was built must have been impregnable—that is, three hundred years ago; but now it could be knocked to pieces with artillery in a very short time, being commanded by several of the neighbouring heights; and from the rear, where it is much lower, running nearly down to the plain, it could be shelled beautifully. An immense deep rocky chasm runs the whole way round, making a splendid natural fosse. The place is of great extent, a good three miles in circumference, if not more. From the walls we had a beautiful view of the surrounding country—a vast heaving ocean of green corn, bounded only by the horizon, through which we could descry the silver waters of the Jhelum winding in the distance, and flashing in the light of the setting sun. It was a landscape that would have done John Company's heart good to gaze on—such a fat, rich, and fertile country, added to his gigantic empire. Few Europeans have set eyes on it before. We are unveiling the arcana of this rich champaign; it has been a sealed volume hitherto, and I hope to have some strange things to relate during my progress. I lose a great deal by not being well at present, and therefore unable to go out sight-seeing. But I trust soon to be all right, and never was invalid more impatient. I am all abroad this month, from not having received letters from home. I look for them every fortnight as regularly as clock-work, and feel most disappointed when I don't receive them. I imagine that my letters from you have been lost. A lot of our mail has been intercepted by the Sikhs this last month, and my letters, probably, were among the number. The verdure of the surrounding countryside almost allows me to think myself at home—what a delusion! Waited till our camels crawled up; made myself comfortable for the night; wrote a little, and went to bed.

March 3—We halt here until the rest of the army arrives, and then, I suppose, we shall push on for Peshawar. Fifty of the enemy's horsemen came in today, and gave themselves up. Poor fellows! they are starving, and had offered their horses for one meal. O war! such are thy trophies! My heart bleeds for the poor wretches. Hunger always with me will cover a multitude of sins; and I believe if the veriest wretch that ever disgraced the human species were to come to me and beg for food, I should pity and relieve him. The enemy are said to be about eighteen miles off, though in what number I know not. Instead of halting for the coming up of the rest of the army, we march on tomorrow.

March 4—Marched at six, ten miles; country very hilly, and intersected with ravines and broken ground, so as to make it extremely difficult for troops to pass. Arrived at our ground about ten, breakfasted, and waited for our tents, which arrived sooner than usual. It is the hottest day we have had yet, and gives us a foretaste of what we are to expect. Sick of being invalided, so reported myself well in the evening. I think, by keeping tolerably quiet, I shall do very well. Shere Singh is trying to make terms for himself, only requiring his life to be insured, and a promise that he shall not be transported. The Sikhs have retreated again at our approach; if they knew how easily they might cut up our brigade and the two batteries, we should be in a very ugly predicament—twelve miles in advance of the whole army, and in a country almost impassable.

March 5—Marched at five, very cold—entered the Borahkee pass. The road lay along the bed of a river—shocking bad ground—perpendicular hills on either side—a beautiful place for an ambush. Marched eight miles and a half, got into our ground early, wrote letters, or rather journal. I am hungering for a letter: I hope I shall receive one soon, or else I lose all spirit. Your letters are the cordials which keep me going from one fortnight to another, and make the time pass pleasantly. Beware how you let me forget home, and home associations: you don't know how important it is, out here, to be kept constantly in mind that there are other ends to live for, nobler than the present hour. If it were not for these recollections, many would become reckless, and care little what became of them.

March 6—Marched at five; entered fresh defile—the scenery magnificent. I wish I could sketch, to give you some idea of the wild grandeur of the mountain defiles we have traversed. The gorge reached for eight miles—the most rough and uneven road we have had yet. At the end of that, we came to the key of the pass, an ascent of a quarter of a mile—almost perpendicular—where only one camel could pass at a time. After we had surmounted this, we came upon a vast plain, intersected with ravines. The artillery had great difficulty in scaling them; the horses were obliged to be taken out, and the guns dragged up by men. It took three hours to get them all to the top. Marched on about two miles, till we were quite clear of the ravines, and then halted. One artilleryman had his leg smashed in three places, by one of the guns breaking loose and running back on him. The enemy are only fourteen miles ahead. All the Sikh infantry have deserted, and they have nothing but cavalry and artillery left. One thousand came in yesterday, and gave up their arms. Major Lawrence and Bowie are in a very critical position. We can never catch these fellows if they fly from us—they go two miles to our one; and if they are hard pressed, the prisoners are at any time liable to be murdered by some fanatic rascal or other. Bowie managed to send a letter in yesterday, saying that they were beginning to be ill-treated, and begging us to make exertions to liberate them. We passed by a village where the Sikhs had blown up a quantity of their ammunition, but not having a correct idea of the power of gunpowder, they had exploded three of themselves and eleven villagers, besides two houses. They were lying about in small bits, arms and legs all blackened and shrivelled, and hardly distinguishable. The Commander-in-Chief's notification appeared yesterday—I see we are mentioned as the only brigade actively engaged. Got some breakfast, and wandered about all day, vainly waiting for our tents; felt very miserable and unwashed. It was very hot too. We had dinner at dusk. It became so cold that we had to walk about to keep ourselves warm until 12 o'clock, when our tents made their appearance. Pitched, and turned in, but alas!—my misfortunes will never cease—my bed was broken to pieces, my chair likewise; and—the unkindest cut of all—a bundle containing the greater portion of my shirts, pocket-handkerchiefs, towels, socks, and white trousers, had been lost on the road, and how I am to replace them I know not; however, I am, as I said before, a philosopher, and in spite of my losses, which are no trifle, I slept.

March 7—Halted. Up at nine, breakfasted, dressed, and went and played a game at cricket—tiffed, and wrote letters. A hundred of the enemy came in and gave up their arms today; a message has been sent to Shere Singh to say, if he carries on the prisoners any further, a price will be put on his head. I fancy this will bring him in.

March 8—Marched at five; the first two miles the road ran through a succession of yawning chasms, ravine after ravine, up and down hill. Such a frightful place you never saw: it took us a good two hours to get through it. But after passing that, it was comparatively easy work—only an occasional hundred yards of ravine. We had to halt, every now and then, to let the artillery get on, which made the march a most tedious one. It was twelve o'clock before we reached our ground, where we found breakfast ready; at two o'clock our tents came up, and it began to rain. We hear that Abbott, with some of Gholab Singh's troops, has taken possession of a pass in front of Shere Singh, and he must now either fight or yield.

Evening—I have just heard that the prisoners, Major and Mrs Lawrence, Herbert, and Bowie, have been sent in, and are now in our camp; if this be the case, we shall probably see Mr Shere himself before long. Five hundred Sikhs came and laid down their arms today. It is raining hard, and it is dinner-time—more certain news tomorrow.

After dinner—It is all true; Major Lawrence, and his wife and two children, Herbert, and Bowie, arrived this evening. Shere Singh comes in tomorrow, and so the campaign with the Sikhs is over. We may have some fighting with the Afghans, but I suspect not. Good night.

March 9—Shere Singh has come into camp—not as a prisoner as yet, but to try and make terms. He wishes to be allowed to send in the guns and arms on *hackeries*, but Gilbert will consent to nothing but the whole army marching by, and depositing the arms at his feet; and to these terms

I believe he has consented, because he can't help himself. But I must go and have a peep. I have seen Shere Singh and the prisoners. Mrs Lawrence and the children appear in excellent health and spirits. How glad she must be to get amongst her own people again! However, I hope her fame will go a great way towards reconciling her to the hardships she has endured. She says that, until the retreat of the Sikhs, when she had to march night and day, she was treated with the greatest consideration and respect, and so were all the rest of the prisoners. Shere Singh is a short, fat, ugly little fellow, very much marked with the smallpox, and as black as your hat. At one o'clock we marched fourteen miles—worse ground than ever; miles of ravines—chasms on either side—here and there a small cultivated spot smiling in the midst of the wilderness; all the rest was a black and barren waste. The sun was fearfully hot. Encamped in an open space near to a large dome, said to be built by Alexander the Great, under which Bucephalus—*credat Judœus*—lies buried! After sunset it became very cold, and we had to wander about, or lie down on the ground, as we pleased, until ten o'clock, before our tents came up. We then got something to satisfy our hunger—it was flesh, and had undergone a sort of operation before the fire, and that is all I can say for it; but we were too hungry to be fastidious. As soon as I had bolted some food, I went to bed, very thankful at having that luxury, instead of sleeping, as we expected, in the open air. It is astonishing what a few things a man really wants. Give me a covering for my head, something to keep me warm, and anything in the shape of food, and I can go on for a long time; but the *sub Jove aperto* work is rather too much of a good thing to make a constant practice of. It may do very well for Harold the Dauntless, and that sort of gentleman, who had a skin like ox-hide, and the constitution of a 24-pounder—who esteemed a stone for a pillow a luxury. Happy fellows, whose luxuries were so cheap! But to delicately-nurtured youths like myself, liable to all the maladies which afflict the human frame, a tent and a bed are almost necessaries. I had a long talk with Shere Singh's head man today, about the action. I asked him, among other things, "where his master was during the fight." He angrily denied the report of his having fled early in the day, and said he was in front of his army the whole time, and had three horses shot under him.

March 10—On duty. Up at seven. Inspected the provisions—which consists in taking a handful of rice, tea, or coffee, in your hands, and pretending to know if it's good or not—looking knowingly at two dozen or so quartered sheep—and breaking a loaf of bread in half, and eating a piece. Marched off my guard, relieved B——, and here I am on my solitary tour of duty at the quarter-guard. We halt today, I am happy to say. We are all glad of a little rest, and prize it the more from the hard work we have had lately. Tomorrow, I believe, or the next day, we enact the last scene of the Sikh campaign, and receive charge of Shere Singh and his remaining guns. Khan Singh is coming in with his followers and fifty *zamborrucks*—a species of small gun, carried on a camel, and holding a pound-ball or so. We are sure now of having to pass the hot weather either at Peshawar or Attock. What we shall do for houses, I don't know; but I suppose there will be some species of dwellings found for us, if the enemy don't destroy them before we arrive—in which case we shall have to dig holes under our beds, and luxuriate there through the heat of the day. Dost Mohammed writes to the governor-general, and hopes that "though appearances are a good deal against him, his excellency will consider him as our sincere friend." The scoundrel! Bowie has got copies of a lot of letters from him to Shere Singh, urging him to join in a crusade to sweep the Feringhees from the country. He has regularly compromised himself with us, and made the Sikhs his enemies by his half measures and the outrages committed at Attock. Parade for the inspection of General Gilbert. We march to-morrow, to receive the Sikh guns in order of battle—a wise precaution, as there is no knowing what treachery these fellows may be meditating. Stayed with my guard all day, and wrote letters—turned out, and fell in with my guard during parade—presented arms to the general, and after that went to see Khan Singh's followers come in. They marched in bodies of two hundred; and each man, as he passed, threw his arms on a heap in front of the general's tent. There were about one thousand of them; and I never saw anything like the reluctance with which they seemed to part with their weapons. Many of them were fine grey-haired old fellows, with large flowing white beards, probably some of Runjeet Singh's veterans. One old fellow I noticed in particular: he stood for a long time looking wistfully at his arms, and the pile before him, and evidently could not make up his mind to give them up. At last the officer on duty came and touched him on the shoulder, and ordered him to move on; he then threw down his sword and matchlock with a crash, and turned away, saying, with tears in his eyes, "All my work is done now." I quite pitied the poor fellow's feelings, and should have liked to give them all their arms back again, had I not known that they would have felt the greatest pleasure in cutting our throats the next minute. After they had deposited their weapons, they went away—goodness knows where—probably without a farthing in their pockets to procure food with. There was an immense pile of muskets, matchlocks, *tulwars*, (native swords,) spears, *zamborrucks*, and six or seven guns of heavier metal, and one ten-inch mortar. As I went away, I met a company of pioneers coming to break up the matchlocks. The swords will probably be sold by auction. Posted sentries, dined, and sat up reading for some time.

March 11—Struck my tent at half-past four. Pouring with rain, and bitterly cold. Joined the regiment, and had to remain drenched and shivering for two hours before we marched. The Bombay column preceded us. We had been told that there was a chance of a fight, and the men were in capital spirits, in spite of the weather. Marched along for eight miles, until we came to a very narrow and difficult pass, where we had to halt in the rain till the Bombay division had passed through. It took us about three hours before we got to the other side of it—the pioneers having to go ahead and clear a road for the guns. All this in a pouring rain was very agreeable, as you may imagine. Hunger, wet, and cold, are great drawbacks to the pleasure of wearing a red jacket, at the time, though they rather enhance it afterwards. I am, for my part, very seldom dull here; marching, bivouacking, fasting—being laid up, wet through, or comfortable—I generally keep up my spirits and laugh at my hardships: *a fortiori*—if I remember right, that's the term in dialectics—should those at home be the very essence of light-heartedness. After we had got through the defile, (I shall be an enemy to hill scenery for life,) we emerged on a small plain surrounded by hills, where we saw our camp, and that of the Sikhs in the distance. Found, to our joy, that the mess-tent was up, the camels having preceded us by a short cut. Got inside, and wrung the wet out of our clothes, as well as we were able, and then made an onslaught on some very suspicious-looking chops. Hunger appeased, I wandered over to see Chuttur and Shere Singh, who had arrived before we came up. Father and son, and all the other Sirdars, were sitting in a circle on a carpet in the general's tent. They seemed quite happy, and were talking and laughing away as if it was quite a joke being prisoners. In the afternoon the guns, twenty-six in number, were brought in: their artillerymen brought them up to the park, unlimbered, dismounted, gave up their swords, and went off. They were all very nice brass pieces, two of them the guns lost at Chilianwalla. The rest of the army come in, I hear, tomorrow. After I had witnessed all that was to be seen, returned to camp. The rain increased into a regular storm at night. The thunder was such as you only hear in India—at times perfectly stunning, and so close that you would fancy you were in the clouds. The lightning lit up every object with a terrible distinctness, and the water poured down like a deluge. Sat up writing for a long time, and enjoying the storm. There is nothing I like better than thunder and lightning, if I am under cover.

March 12—About one o'clock was gladdened by receiving the long-expected overland. I need not say what pleasure it gave me. Five thousand Sikhs laid down their arms in camp today; the rest come in tomorrow. By the bye, I forgot to tell you of a conversation I had with a Sikh yesterday. I was asking him questions about the battle. He said, "he knew nothing about it, except what happened in the village."

"Oh, you were in the village, were you?" said I; "why didn't you hold it?"

"Well," replied my friend, "what was the use?—the Europeans came on us like so many devils, and seemed determined to have it—so we ran; what could we do?"

"It was the best thing you could have done," said I.

With which anecdote, illustrative of native *savoir vivre,* I will conclude for the present.

Camp, Rawalpindi

Chapter 7

March to Attock and Peshawar

March 13, Rawalpindi—Struck our tents at 4 a.m., and waited outside for a couple of hours, when an order came down countermanding the march until twelve o'clock, as the river was too much swollen by the two last days to be fordable. Re-pitched one tent, and lay down again. At twelve we marched, I went along in a *doolie*: by the bye, you don't know what a *doolie* is? It is a rude kind of *palkee*, very light, made for the purpose of carrying the sick, and borne by four men; has a cane bottom, and is open at the top and sides, over which a cloth is thrown to protect you from the sun. Altogether it looks very much like a coffin. Reached the banks of the river—a swift stream running over a rocky bed, at the foot of a barren range of hills. Here I had to get out and ride across. Thousands of the Sikhs met us on our march, going to lay down their arms. It was strange to see us passing so coolly and indifferently those with whom, but a short time back, we were waging war to the knife,—jostling one another in the ford, and, without looking, brushing by those whom, a week ago, you would only have approached sword in hand. Every man, as he reached our side of the ford, deposited his arms on an immense heap that lay on the bank. The reluctance of one poor fellow to part with his *tulwar* quite affected me. After he had thrown it down, he came and prostrated himself, *à la Hindustan,* at the feet of the officer on duty at the pile, and begged, in the most pathetic manner, to have his sword back again. Of course it could not be done—and heaven only knows what atrocities he may have perpetrated with it. After we had crossed the ford, we had to ascend the range of hills; and as there was only one narrow pass crowded with troops, I made my bearers deploy to the left, and discovered a precarious sort of path just practicable. Got out of my *doolie* again, and scrambled up as well as I could to the summit, leaving my bearers to follow. The scene, when I had reached it, was superb— our division of the army crossing the river, and winding along the plain—the Sikhs trooping slowly in, and throwing their weapons on the glittering pile, which shone like silver in the bright sunshine—the Bombay camp pitched at a short distance—(you don't know what a picturesque thing a camp is)—and all around, the black wild mountains, with bright green patches of cultivation in their bosom. It was a most beautiful and novel sight—one to remember and admire, but not to be described. Sat down on the top of the crags, and gazed upon the scene below, until my *doolie* toiled up to the top. Numbers of the Sikhs passed me in my wild and lonely situation,—but we did not molest one another—great forbearance on my part, seeing I was unarmed. The country at the top was flat, and cultivated for a few miles, when there was another bleak range of hills. This is a regular land of mountains. Got into my *doolie*, and, leaving the regiment in the pleasant occupation of dragging the captured guns up the steep road, proceeded to the camp, which was only a short distance a-head. It was a most lovely afternoon,—a sweet fresh wind blowing over the mountains, and filling one's mind with visions of home. Found my tent had arrived by a different road; had it pitched and went to bed; spent the evening alone, drank tea, and read the despatch, which has come out. It is wonderfully true—without even excusable exaggeration. However, this is not needed; the results speak for themselves. The Chief, I see, gives the credit of storming the village to the *whole* brigade. General Gilbert has done *us* justice, and states that it was stormed in a gallant manner by the 2nd Europeans, with *only* the loss of eight killed, and 135 wounded. The number who have since died makes the number up to twenty, with poor Sprot: and very many of the wounded, I am sorry to say, are disabled for life. The Sikh guns that we have in camp amount to 36: two of them are French guns with the Paris mark on them, and quite new; kind of our friends across the Channel! I can scarcely get beyond a guess of the number of the enemy who have given up their arms, but I should say about 15,000. A number of them object to doing so, and we march tomorrow to bring them to their senses. So good-night—To sleep!

March 14—Marched at eight; beautiful day. After about three miles, came to the Sikh camp. As anticipated, the sight of us brought them to submission, and they are bringing in their arms as fast as possible. By evening, they had all deposited them, and the country was covered for miles with the dispersing multitude. We found an immense quantity of ammunition in their camp, which was all blown up. The place we are at now, Rawalpindi, is celebrated for the manufacture of cloth. All the *dák* packages, that have been lost during the campaign, were found in a magazine here. We shall be at Peshawar in little more than a fortnight, if Dost Mohammed does not make a fool of himself. There we shall get very decent quarters—apples and grapes too, and ice from the surrounding mountains.

March 15—I have now passed my two years' service. It seems more like twenty when I look back to my first landing, and more like a month when I think of my leaving home—so vividly do I remember everything connected with that melancholy occasion. Last Christmas was my third away from home—how often I recollect the last there, and pray that I may spend many more such. A protecting Providence has watched over me so far: may it please God to continue it unto the end. They are sad things, these breakings up of family circles—these tearings asunder of those who, from childhood, have been knit together in the bonds of love—but it must be so. Tents struck at three o'clock—marched at four—a long march of seventeen miles—country very fertile, and road good, with the exception of an occasional ravine, or dry bed of a river; the plain covered with a small bright purple flower, which looked very beautiful. In the last two miles, we entered a low jungle, at the foot of a range of hills, abounding in game—deer, partridges, and hares—reached our ground about twelve. We are pitched in the jungle at the foot of the hills, through which we shall have to pass tomorrow. The Bombay division follow—one march behind. We have only three marches to make to Attock now. The Sikhs have all given in—some 25,000—and 38 guns. Shere and his respected parent are in camp. The heads of the rebellion are spared, and will probably be pensioned for life; while the miserable instruments are turned adrift, penniless and starving, to seek their distant homes—or else have fallen in the senseless contest. These Indian princes never pay their troops, except in cases of victory; and as they are always licked, the deluded soldiers never get paid at all.

March 16—Turned out at half-past three; started at five. The country about here is the most beautiful I have seen in India—hill and dale thickly covered with wood, and all in one purple glow from the carpet of flowers which entirely hides the earth. Entered the pass between the hills which Abbott had so opportunely taken possession of; and after three hours or so fighting one's way through camels, horses, and men, emerged on the plain on the other side. Marched sixteen miles,—did not reach our ground until one o'clock. And now, just as we have swallowed some food, washed, and begin to feel comfortable, we are told that we are to march at eight o'clock tonight, and push on to Attock, a distance of thirty-six miles. Jolly—very! Dost Mohammed, they say, is burning the boats, and we wish to spoil his sport—very natural on his part, and on ours.

After news—We march at six instead of eight, and there is every chance of a tight scrimmage. Dost Mohammed is trying to cross; and, if we catch him in the act, he must fight. I wish we had another European corps with us. The doctor strongly recommends my staying behind—but I can't run the risk of the regiment being engaged and I away. I had rather lose a limb: and so I am to go, and be answerable, or rather responsible, for the consequences. So good-bye for the present.

March 17—Here I am at Attock, after a night and day of such fatigue and discomfort as I have seldom passed before. But it is pleasant to look back on labours over. And now that I am comfortable again, I would not have missed the march for the world. We started yesterday at six o'clock p. m., and went the whole night at the rate of little more than a mile an hour, the roads being so bad that the artillery could make no progress, and we had but little moonlight. I don't know anything more tedious and fatiguing than sitting on horseback, and crawling along at that pace. The inclination to sleep is painful in the extreme. Time after time, I nearly fell off my saddle. It was intensely cold, and I had nothing but my cloak. I would have given worlds to have been allowed to walk. In this miserable way, we mooned away for twelve miles, and then halted for a couple of hours. Threw myself on the ground, and was asleep in a second. It seemed scarcely two minutes before we had to start again, and it required all my resolution to make me to quit my hard couch. After this, we marched on all night, and until ten o'clock next morning, when we halted, having accomplished twenty-six miles. The sun was very powerful, and I was obliged to resort to my old expedient of hanging my cloak on my sword, under which I devoured the loaf of bread we each had for breakfast, and then fell fast asleep. At twelve o'clock we had to post off again—awfully hot—the men keeping up bravely; only a few fell out, from sheer inability to proceed, and were put on elephants. The road was very good at this part of the march, and we got along splendidly. The fertility of the country wonderful—the eye can rest on no spot which is not covered with green corn. All over the plain, as far as we could see, to the foot of the hills, which shut it in on all sides, it was one mass of cultivation. Verily, it is a goodly land. General Gilbert went ahead with the cavalry and horse-artillery; and after we had been marching about two hours, we heard firing for a short time. Ten miles brought us to the end of our march, on the banks of the celebrated Indus, and in possession of Attock. At General Gilbert's approach with the cavalry, the Afghans, after firing two or three shots, fled across the river by the bridge of boats, leaving three of their guns, and commenced burning the boats, to prevent our following. They had half completed the work of destruction, when Captain Fordyce's troop came up, and opened upon them across the river with grape, which they returned from a few guns, but soon retired out of range. We have saved half the boats, and so have got something by our forced march. Some of the troops were put in the fort to hold it, and we encamped outside. I have not yet seen Attock, as we are pitched in such a position that a bend in the hills conceals it from our view. Our tents arrived shortly after us, and by sunset we were once more comfortable. General Gilbert was pleased to compliment us on our marching, and justly so; for thirty-six miles, with sixteen before it, is very good work. Got some dinner at seven, and here I am drinking tea, and giving you an account of my labours. I am not the least the worse for the exercise, which is very lucky, as I might have done myself a great deal of injury. We have got possession of Attock, and, I hope, shall halt tomorrow before we do anything else. Dost Mohammed is at the other side of the river, with, it is said, twelve guns, and 10,000 men though I scarcely think he can have the impudence to think of meeting us with such a force. That our *best friend* intends to resist, there is little doubt, from his destroying the boats, and firing on us today. And now, good-night! as you won't be surprised when I tell you I am tired.

Sunday, March 18—We halt today, thank goodness—for we are very much in need of rest. I have had a good night's sleep, and feel rather the better for the march. This has been a campaign with a vengeance; and, as —— says, if they give a year's *batta* for Chilianwalla and Gujarat, the troops that crossed the Jhelum ought to get two years. It is very hot here; I hope it will not be our summer quarters.

Evening—I have been luxuriating in idleness all day—writing a little, reading a little, yawning a great deal, and listening listlessly to whatever news my friends were good enough to tell me. The bridge of boats is completed by this time. We offered the villagers a hundred rupees for every boat they brought us; and by this means, with those taken, managed to get sufficient to reach across. We march to-morrow, and are to make Peshawar in three marches. The Khyberees, or inhabitants of the Khyber pass, have sold it to us. To understand this, I must tell you, if so be you don't know, that the natives of that portion of the earth, taking advantage of their position, levy a black-mail on all who pass through; and as the only entrance into Afghanistan is by that infernal hole, it is to be supposed they net a very considerable income. Dost Mohammed bought his passage to this side with 10,000 rupees, and we have bribed the chief of the Khyberees with a *lac*—10,000 down, and the British word for the rest—not to let him through again. He has agreed to this, but says that he cannot hold the pass against guns, if Dost Mohammed choose to force it; but if we move on as fast as possible, he will keep him in check till we come up; so it may be hoped we have the enemy in a trap, and he must either fight or yield. We shall have some long marches, though,—the enemy having retreated last night, and being a long way off by this time. I fancy they would bolt altogether, if they could. It is five regular marches to Peshawar, but I suppose we shall do it in less than that. Forced marching seems the order of the day—and the general is so pleased with ours of the last two days, that he is very likely to give us some more of it.

March 19—Marched at six; passed under Attock; halted at the bridge of boats. The guns were crossing at the time; and as the bridge was very bad, and very narrow, we had to wait about three hours before we could attempt the passage; during which time I amused myself by taking an observation of Attock, wandering round the base of the rock on which it is situated, and throwing pebbles into the Indus. I was rather disappointed in Attock: it is a common Indian fort, built on the top of a black rock, and surrounded on all sides by the river, but not at all a strong place. It is commanded by every hill around it; and the only advantage it seems to possess, is commanding the crossing of the river. It is very dirty and hot withal. The Indus must be a splendid river in the rains; but now it is much sunken, very deep and strong, and rushes with awful rapidity through its rocky channel, forming a hundred eddies and small whirlpools. The sun was very hot before we began to cross, which took us an hour. We then halted on the other side; the men got their breakfasts and we did ditto. The reflection of the sun from the rocks was almost intolerable. After halting for an hour or so, we marched, and entered another of those horrid passes, the worst I have seen yet—very narrow and steep, and very disagreeable to me, as I was riding a friend's horse, which had given way in the loins, and every time there was a crush, and I was obliged to stand still, he give way in the hind-quarters, and almost sat down. The beauty of the scenery, however, more than atoned for this unpleasant way of viewing it: on either side there was a grassy slope strewed with flowers, forming a soft contrast to the black hills which rose, frowning one over the other, all around. The pass was three miles long; and at the end of it we halted for some time, by a delicious cool spring under the shadow of some trees. Dismounted, bathed my face and hands; and (excuse the offence) lighting my *meerschaum,* stretched myself under the shade of a palm-tree, and luxuriated in the complacent meditations ever inspired by the soothing weed. After a pleasant halt, went on again, gained the plain, and came in sight of the Kabul river, which joins the Indus somewhere near. The road ran along about two hundred yards from its banks; and finding it very hot and dusty riding with the regiment, I fell to the rear, turned off the road, and sat down under a tree for about an hour, when a lot of suspicious-looking personages prowling about the hill over my head, with matchlocks, told me it would be advisable to proceed. Mounted my horse, and, crossing the road, followed leisurely along the banks of the river—and truly there was good excuse for any admirer of nature to loiter. The plain for miles was clothed with green grass, (an unprecedented sight in India) and nothing could equal the gorgeous beauty of the carpet of purple flowers which adorned it. It seemed as if you were looking at everything through a richly-stained piece of glass—and the perfume springing from it was most delicious. For miles I rode dreaming on, lost in sweet visions of home and England, until I came to a scene that changed these pleasant feelings. A number of our camp-followers were plundering the crops of an unfortunate old villager, destroying the wood-work of his well, and carrying away all the little the poor man had, utterly regardless of his tears and supplications; and when I came up, the old fellow threw himself flat on his face before me, and besought me in the most piteous manner to save his all from being taken from him. I had a heavy-thonged hunting-whip in my hand; and didn't I lay it about me! The blackguards dispersed like lightning; but that wasn't the thing at all. I cantered after each, and thrashed him till he yelled, until I had gone through them all, brought them back, and made them restore everything they had plundered; and then, with a few final cuts, sent them about their business. The poor old gentleman was very grateful; but a good deal of damage had been done that I could not repair. After that, I rode over to a village to get a drink of water; and while it was being hoisted up from the well, I got as much information as I could from the villagers. Dost Mohammed had passed by, they said, only the day before, with seven or eight guns, and some ten thousand men. Cantered after the regiment, which was some four miles ahead; passed them, and rode into camp, where I found the mess-tent up. The march today was fifteen miles. It was sunset when we arrived on our ground; got dinner at seven, and had to wait till half-past ten before my tent made its appearance, when I lost no time in getting to bed—very tired, as you may suppose, from being the whole day in the sun.

March 20—Stayed behind, and saw everything packed and under weigh, and then rode quietly along the road by myself. The mornings are most delightful up here—cool, fresh air, like the hills; while down in the plains, we hear, they have got *punkahs*.

March 21—Turned out at twelve last night, and marched at one; very dark at first starting, but our eyes soon got accustomed to the light, and we got along capitally. The road was surprisingly good. Walked till daylight without stopping, and then halted for half an hour; lay down on the ground, and breakfasted off a sandwich. Went on again, and the men got over the ground splendidly until about the sixteenth mile, when the sun became overpoweringly hot, and they began to look dreadfully distressed. However, there was no sign of flagging; and though, even on horse-back, I felt regularly seared, the plucky little fellows strode along with unabated energy: but their reeking brows and limping gait told plainly that there was very little more go in them. Anything like the heat I have not felt yet. About eleven we came in sight of Peshawar, and reached it at twelve. It is an ugly native city, surrounded with high mud walls, and very uninteresting to the eye. All the gates were closed by order of the general, to prevent plunder, and therefore we could not see the inside. Marched round the walls, and rested beneath them on the other side of the town for about an hour, where we all, officers and men, regaled ourselves with handfuls of dates, which were sold in great abundance, and very cheap. We then moved on two more miles to our encamping ground, which we reached at three o'clock, after a march of at least twenty-eight miles. The men are completely done up; they cannot do much more: it is not so much the distance, as the time they are out, and the little rest they have had lately. They are almost all foot-sore—and what makes it more painful to see is, that they never grumble, but would march on, I believe, till their legs dropped off. By Jove! when you read in books of such and such a general having advanced rapidly by vigorous forced marches, you have but a very vague idea, or rather a thought never enters one's head, of what the poor devils of soldiers suffered from that same energetic move, by which the general got so much kudos. General Gilbert was much pleased with the men, so we have our reward—more than enough for us, to whom a few words of praise is a recompense for any hardship. Jack's friend, "General"—(I cannot make out his name) is a very sensible fellow. The 2nd Europeans *is* "the smartest and most active regiment in India," and I am proud to belong to it. Lay in the sun grilling for two hours before the baggage arrived; got a loaf of bread and two eggs; and here I am, after having enjoyed a good bathe, once more comfortable, and at charity with all men. I fancy now the campaign is over, and that we shall be allowed to repose under our laurels—which, by the way, are the only shelter we shall have for some time, for not the suspicion of a house is there here fit for a European; that scoundrel of an Afghan has burnt them all. We passed the smoking ruins of the cantonments on our march, and Major Lawrence's house, a fine old palace, utterly destroyed. Imagine me, when you get this, inhabiting something in the wigwam style—stick, dirt, and mats. It will be a very good climate, however; the sun is powerful, but the mornings and evenings are cool, and under shelter we shan't want *punkahs*. There are lots of apples, pears, grapes, plums, and green peas. I had a beautiful bouquet brought me today, roses, mignionette, wallflowers, and poppies. They seemed like old friends, and called up so many pleasant and sad recollections. Some say we (*i. e.* our brigade) are to go back to Rawalpindi, and build cantonments there. For my part, I don't care where we go, as long as we have a little rest. We are at least at the end of our tether for the present, and heartily glad we all are of it. I believe, however, Dost Mohammed has got through the pass. I haven't told you yet what the Sikhs have called our regiment. Some of them, when they came in the other day, inquired which was the corps which stormed the village, and ours being pointed out, said we were a *Shitan ha pultun*—a regiment of devils. Rather complimentary in our friends. A subscription was set on foot the other day for the orphans and widows of the soldiers who fell in the late actions; and yesterday I read in the paper an advertisement from the chaplain, Mr Whiting, saying he had already received such a large sum on their behalf that nothing more was needed, and requesting the public to suspend their charity until he should have occasion to call on them again. No bad trait this of the Indian public.

March 22—I hear from those who have been inside the city (Peshawar) that it is a very fine one; but I will wait till I see it myself, and then give you an account of it, which I shall soon be able to do, as I am nearly well now. We wait here, I believe, for the Chiefs orders. Dost Mohammed is through the pass, but I suspect we have not done with him: however, that's for wiser heads than mine to determine.

March 23—Marched at four to change ground. Stayed behind and rode back to Peshawar; went through one of the gates and out of the other. It is one of the finest native cities I have seen, with the exception of Delhi. The streets are broad and not remarkably filthy, bazaars extensive, lots of shops and houses altogether of a better description than the generality of nigger abodes. The inhabitants are very fair, and have quite a colour in their cheeks; the women are some of them very good-looking. Having stared my fill, I cantered after the army. There had been a heavy fall of rain in the night, and the country was a regular swamp. In leaping over a broad ditch, my horse fell back, and I slipped over the tail up to my waist in water; scrambled out and dragged him after me, and cantered on about four miles to the encampment ground; had to wait two hours while they were marking it out, during which time it came on to rain. The mess-tent was pitched about eleven, and we got breakfast at twelve. Waited another hour before my tent made its appearance, changed my clothes, and got into bed. We are encamped close under the hills, and a few miles from the entrance of the Khyber pass. I am a little feverish from the effects of my ducking, but a night's rest will set me all right again. The hills about us are swarming with a horde of most bloodthirsty and unscrupulous robbers; a number of camp-followers have been stripped and murdered, and there is an order against going beyond the pickets, and staying in the city after dark. Patrols are established all along the roads, and the sentries have orders to fire on everyone who approaches their post after sunset. These unprincipled gentry hold the neutral ground, and rob, murder, and prey on all who come within their reach; so we shall have to go about well armed whilst we stay here. By the bye, I have a little trait of national viciousness for you. I noticed this morning my little page, a small boy, son of my bearer, seemingly rejoicing over two tame quails that he had bought. I was rather pleased to see anything like the characteristics of childhood in the little urchin—the generality of them grow so prematurely old and wicked—so I called him to me, and asked what he intended to do with them.

"Oh," said the precocious youth, (he is about twelve,) "I shall keep them till they are a little older, and then they'll fight capitally."

There was the innocence of childhood for you! I have never introduced my small page to you before. He is a remarkably smart boy—does as much work as two men—is very much attached to me—always at hand—and rejoices in the name of Latonman. His old father is in his dotage, so the little fellow does all the work—superintends everything, dresses me, runs messages, takes care of my clothes—in fact does everything, and isn't more addicted to lying, stealing, and cheating, than the rest of his race. The accounts the Sikhs give of the battle of Gujarat is rather amusing. They say that, for the first three hours, the fire on them from our guns was *ardens quasi infernum,* and almost took away their breath; and at last, when it slackened, and they rose up, they saw six miles of infantry advancing on them: "What was the use of stopping after that?"

March 24—It is deliciously cool after the rain. What a contrast this climate is to the burning heat of the plains! I trust we shall keep the country; we then shall have some more good stations, where a European can call his existence living. I was rather surprised yesterday by the seeming poverty of a large city like Peshawar, but now that is explained. All the rich merchants were so alarmed for their property, during the time that the Sikhs and Afghan army were encamped here, that they buried their goods. A short time will reassure them of our peaceful intentions, and then we shall see something of the celebrated merchandise of the city. Spent my morning as usual. I am very tired of being an invalid. I believe we are nearly sure to get the medal and *batta*: I hope it is so; they will both be very acceptable.

Sunday, March 25—Stayed at home all day.

March 26—There is no news in the camp, except that we have got fever, dysentery, and scurvy among the troops, and particularly in our regiment; the latter will soon be removed by the fruit and vegetables so abundant here. But it would be a melancholy thing to look back some ten years on any European corps in this country, and see how few, how very few, are left. The average of life is hardly ten years. Cholera, liver, apoplexy, battle, and intemperance, make sad ravages amongst us; and the greater number of those who put foot on these shores never leave them again. The 61st Queen's came up yesterday, to supply the place of her Majesty's 29th Regiment. The Bombay division is halted two marches from here—the troops too exhausted to come on without rest. Captain Mackenzie of ours was nearly captured today, by some of these Afreydees, or mountain robbers. He was riding out towards Jamrood, a fort a few miles off, and a number of them surrounded him. One collared him, and another seized the bridle; but, being a powerful man, he easily shook off his assailants, put spurs to his horse, and escaped. Amused myself all day with playing on a small Sikh fife, which emits the most doleful squeaks, and annoys the camp excessively. I have had at least six deputations begging me to desist. That, and studying Field's *Exercises and Evolutions of the Army* (a sweet book), have formed my day's occupation. I shall become a smart officer, *nolens volens,* here, as this is the only book in the camp I don't know by heart. There is a report now, that we are to go back again to the provinces. Ground is being marked out for a cantonment here, and at Wuzeerabad they are already building; but it is rumoured that the 2nd Europeans go to Lahore. I am afraid it is too good news to be true.

March 27—It is a lovely day, but getting rather hot, though we still require bed-clothes at night. We hear that Subhatoo is to be done away with as a station, not being considered healthy for Europeans. Oh, the sharp-sightedness of these medical men! True, we lost a good many men up there—but how many more should we have lost in the plains? The overland news is in today: I see in the *Illustrated News* some very dashing pictures of the charge of the 14th Dragoons at Ramnuggur, Shere Singh's bodyguard, &c. How I long to hear what they say of Chilianwalla. We are put to great straits here at present. We have not had any pay issued for three months, and provisions are very dear. The bazaar expenses in the mess alone amount to eighty rupees a month; and our servants hardly get food enough to keep them alive.

March 29—We had such a fearful storm last night, that I was obliged to go to bed before I finished my packet. The candle was blown out—the tent bulged in like a sail—the wind rushed in at every corner—the papers flew out at the door—the tea-pot, cups, and milk-bottle were trundled off the table—everything in the tent rocked and vibrated; and there was nothing for it but creeping into bed, and shivering under the clothes. However, this occurrence enables me to give you the latest news. It is settled that we go back to Lahore, which I am very glad of. It is a nice station; and there are quarters built by government for officers. It is thirty marches from here to Lahore, so we shall not be there before May. Awfully hot it will be, but heat I rather like. Excuse the disreputable appearance of this packet. I wonder how I ever manage to write at all. You should see my table; it requires innumerable tent-pegs to keep it up; and has been repaired time after time, till it has as much cordage about it as a seventy-four. My chair is one mass of rope, and *minus* the back; and my bed has been mended so often that, from being originally made for a man six feet four, it has dwindled down to a place on which one of moderate dimensions finds it difficult to coil up. The tent is the best thing we have got, and that belongs to a friend, and is not impervious to either wind or water. Good-by to you all! God bless you!

Publisher's Note

Ensign Daniel A. Sandford died in the Punjab only twelve weeks after his last journal entry— he was just 19 years and 10 months old. He is buried in Lahore, his grave marked by a mon-umnet erected by his brother officers:

SACRED TO THE MEMORY OF
ENSIGN DANIEL A. SANDFORD
HONBLE CO: 2ND EUROPEAN REGIMENT
WHO DEPARTED THIS LIFE
ON THE 20TH JUNE 1849
AGED 19 YEARS AND 10 MONTHS

THIS TOMB WAS ERECTED BY
HIS BROTHER OFFICERS

LEONAUR

ALSO FROM LEONAUR
AVAILABLE IN SOFTCOVER OR HARDCOVER WITH DUST JACKET

SEPOYS, SIEGE & STORM *by Charles John Griffiths*—The Experiences of a young officer of H.M.'s 61st Regiment at Ferozepore, Delhi ridge and at the fall of Delhi during the Indian mutiny 1857.

CAMPAIGNING IN ZULULAND *by W. E. Montague*—Experiences on campaign during the Zulu war of 1879 with the 94th Regiment.

THE STORY OF THE GUIDES *by G. J. Younghusband*—The Exploits of the Soldiers of the famous Indian Army Regiment from the northwest frontier 1847 - 1900..

ZULU: 1879 *by D.C.F. Moodie & the Leonaur Editors*—The Anglo-Zulu War of 1879 from contemporary sources: First Hand Accounts, Interviews, Dispatches, Official Documents & Newspaper Reports.

THE RECOLLECTIONS OF SKINNER OF SKINNER'S HORSE *by James Skinner*—James Skinner and his 'Yellow Boys' Irregular cavalry in the wars of India between the British, Mahratta, Rajput, Mogul, Sikh & Pindarree Forces.

TOMMY ATKINS' WAR STORIES 14 FIRST HAND ACCOUNTS—Fourteen first hand accounts from the ranks of the British Army during Queen Victoria's Empire Original & True Battle Stories Recollections of the Indian Mutiny With the 49th in the Crimea With the Guards in Egypt The Charge of the Six Hundred With Wolseley in Ashanti Alma, Inkermann and Magdala With the Gunners at Tel-el-Kebir Russian Guns and Indian Rebels Rough Work in the Crimea In the Maori Rising Facing the Zulus From Sebastopol to Lucknow Sent to Save Gordon On the March to Chitral Tommy by Rudyard Kipling

CHASSEUR OF 1914 *by Marcel Dupont*—Experiences of the twilight of the French Light Cavalry by a young officer during the early battles of the great war in Europe.

TROOP HORSE & TRENCH *by R. A. Lloyd*—The experiences of a British Lifeguardsman of the household cavalry fighting on the western front during the First World War 1914-18.

THE EAST AFRICAN MOUNTED RIFLES *by C. J. Wilson*—Experiences of the campaign in the East African bush during the First World War.

THE FIGHTING CAMELIERS *by Frank Reid*—The exploits of the Imperial Camel Corps in the desert and Palestine campaigns of the First World War.

LEONAUR

ALSO FROM LEONAUR

AVAILABLE IN SOFTCOVER OR HARDCOVER WITH DUST JACKET

THE COMPLEAT RIFLEMAN HARRIS *by Benjamin Harris as told to & transcribed by Captain Henry Curling*—The adventures of a soldier of the 95th (Rifles) during the Peninsular Campaign of the Napoleonic Wars

WITH WELLINGTON'S LIGHT CAVALRY *by William Tomkinson*—The Experiences of an officer of the 16th Light Dragoons in the Peninsular and Waterloo campaigns of the Napoleonic Wars.

SERGEANT BOURGOGNE *by Adrien Bourgogne*—With Napoleon's Imperial Guard in the Russian Campaign and on the Retreat from Moscow 1812 - 13.

SWORDS OF HONOUR *by Henry Newbolt & Stanley L. Wood*—The Careers of Six Outstanding Officers from the Napoleonic Wars, the Wars for India and the American Civil War, with dozens of illustrations by Stanley L. Wood.

SURTEES OF THE RIFLES *by William Surtees*—A Soldier of the 95th (Rifles) in the Peninsular campaign of the Napoleonic Wars.

ENSIGN BELL IN THE PENINSULAR WAR *by George Bell*—The Experiences of a young British Soldier of the 34th Regiment 'The Cumberland Gentlemen' in the Napoleonic wars.

HUSSAR IN WINTER *by Alexander Gordon*—A British Cavalry Officer during the retreat to Corunna in the Peninsular campaign of the Napoleonic Wars.

NAPOLEONIC WAR STORIES *by Sir Arthur Quiller-Couch*—Tales of soldiers, spies, battles & sieges from the Peninsular & Waterloo campaingns.

JOURNALS OF ROBERT ROGERS OF THE RANGERS *by Robert Rogers*—The exploits of Rogers & the Rangers in his own words during 1755-1761 in the French & Indian War.

KERSHAW'S BRIGADE VOLUME 1 *by D. Augustus Dickert*—Manassas, Seven Pines, Sharpsburg (Antietam), Fredricksburg, Chancellorsville, Gettysburg, Chickamauga, Chattanooga, Fort Sanders & Bean Station..

KERSHAW'S BRIGADE VOLUME 2 *by D. Augustus Dickert*—At the wilderness, Cold Harbour, Petersburg, The Shenandoah Valley and Cedar Creek.

A TIGER ON HORSEBACK *by L. March Phillips*—The Experiences of a Trooper & Officer of Rimington's Guides - The Tigers - during the Anglo-Boer war 1899 - 1902.

LEONAUR

ALSO FROM LEONAUR
AVAILABLE IN SOFTCOVER OR HARDCOVER WITH DUST JACKET

CAPTAIN OF THE 95th (Rifles) *by Jonathan Leach*—An officer of Wellington's Sharpshooters during the Peninsular, South of France and Waterloo Campaigns of the Napoleonic Wars.

THE KHAKEE RESSALAH *by Robert Henry Wallace Dunlop*—Service & adventure with the Meerut volunteer horse during the Indian mutiny 1857-1858

BUGLER AND OFFICER OF THE RIFLES *by William Green & Harry Smith* With the 95th (Rifles) during the Peninsular & Waterloo Campaigns of the Napoleonic Wars

BAYONETS, BUGLES AND BONNETS *by James 'Thomas' Todd*—Experiences of hard soldiering with the 71st Foot - the Highland Light Infantry - through many battles of the Napoleonic wars including the Peninsular & Waterloo Campaigns

A NORFOLK SOLDIER IN THE FIRST SIKH WAR *by J W Baldwin*—Experiences of a private of H.M. 9th Regiment of Foot in the battles for the Punjab, India 1845-46

A CAVALRY OFFICER DURING THE SEPOY REVOLT *by A.R.D. Mackenzie*—Experiences with the 3rd Bengal Light Cavalry, the Guides and Sikh Irregular Cavalry from the outbreak to Delhi and Lucknow

THE ADVENTURES OF A LIGHT DRAGOON *by George Farmer & G.R. Gleig*—A cavalryman during the Peninsular & Waterloo Campaigns, in captivity & at the siege of Bhurtpore, India

THE COMPLEAT RIFLEMAN HARRIS *by Benjamin Harris as told to & transcribed by Captain Henry Curling*—The adventures of a soldier of the 95th (Rifles) during the Peninsular Campaign of the Napoleonic Wars

THE RED DRAGOON *by W.J. Adams*—With the 7th Dragoon Guards in the Cape of Good Hope against the Boers & the Kaffir tribes during the 'war of the axe' 1843-48

THE LIFE OF THE REAL BRIGADIER GERARD - Volume 1 - THE YOUNG HUSSAR 1782 - 1807 *by Jean-Baptiste De Marbot*—A French Cavalryman Of the Napoleonic Wars at Marengo, Austerlitz, Jena, Eylau & Friedland

THE LIFE OF THE REAL BRIGADIER GERARD Volume 2 IMPERIAL AIDE-DE-CAMP 1807 - 1811 *by Jean-Baptiste De Marbot*—A French Cavalryman of the Napoleonic Wars at Saragossa, Landshut, Eckmuhl, Ratisbon, Aspern-Essling, Wagram, Busaco & Torres Vedras

Lightning Source UK Ltd.
Milton Keynes UK
24 February 2010

150545UK00001B/25/A